Praise

I have had the great opportunity to hear Jeff speak and his book provides more detail and background on how he has reached such achievements in his life. The chapters are really nice vignettes with a life lesson that can be read and shared one at a time. The book is motivating and would be great to share with your kids or co-workers when talking about being true to yourself and pushing through adversity. Inspirational!
D. L.

As I read I found myself totally engrossed. It was captivating, full of suspense and adventure....MountainVision should be mandatory reading for every student, every teacher, every sports team, every business group, congregation, military unit, police department, and in short, every parent and every child.
J. D.

This book was riveting, and awe-inspiring. When I finally put it down, I felt inspired and am able to see life through a different lens. Jeff delivers his core messages so artistically, and in a way that inspires you to improve the way you live your life. My view of humanity, the nature of the human spirit, and of the core values gained from taking chances and living life to its fullest are forever changed. I learned valuable life lessons with each chapter that can apply to avid outdoor enthusiasts and urban adventure seekers alike.
J. H.

I heard about this book after Jeff and his team were on the show Expedition Impossible, *and I fell in love with their spirit. I could not put the book down. I found it funny, inspiring, riveting, dramatic, funny again ...I found myself laughing right out loud many times. But what I found most incredible is how he gives such praise to everyone around him and doesn't seem to take credit for anything good that happens around him. He wants everyone around him to be successful!*
S.W.

MOUNTAINVISION

LESSONS BEYOND THE SUMMIT

JEFF B. EVANS

TwP

Touchwood Press
Arlington Heights, Illinois

Copyright © 2007, 2016, 2017 by Jeff B. Evans. All rights reserved.

No part of this book may be reproduced or transmitted in any form or by any means, electronic or mechanical, including photocopying, recording, or by an information storage and retrieval system, except by a reviewer who may quote brief passages in a review, without permission in writing. Contact touchwoodpress@gmail.com.

Although the author and publisher have made every effort to ensure the accuracy and completeness of information contained in this book, we assume no responsibility for errors, inaccuracies, omissions, or any inconsistency herein. Any slights of people, places, or organizations are unintentional.

Published by TOUCHWOOD PRESS
September 2019
touchwoodpress.com

Printed and bound in the United States of America.

Cover photo by Didrik Johnck, johnck.com
Cover design by pro_ebookcovers
Editing by Adrian Vigliano

ISBN-13: 978-1-946313-05-8

Visit the author's website at http://jeffbevans.com for information about obtaining signed copies of this book. To inquire about volume discounts and special requirements, contact the publisher at touchwoodpress@gmail.com.

CONTENTS

PREFACE
FOREWORD BY ERIK WEIHENMAYER

PART I: CLIMBING MOUNTAINS 15
CHAPTER 1: NEVER LET GO 18
CHAPTER 2: NEVER STOP SEEKING 22
CHAPTER 3: THE RIGHT FIT 38
CHAPTER 4: TRAINING WHEELS 45
CHAPTER 5: LEARNING TO LEAD 56
CHAPTER 6: SOUTH AMERICA 91
CHAPTER 7: RACING RUGGED 95
CHAPTER 8: PRIMAL QUEST 100
CHAPTER 9: THINKING BIG 107

PART II: EXPEDITION IMPOSSIBLE 132
CHAPTER 10: THE COMPETITION 134
CHAPTER 11: LEAVING ERIK BEHIND 137
CHAPTER 12: IF HE'S WILLING TO PUSH IT, I'M WILLING TO TAKE HIM THERE 138
CHAPTER 13: IF YOU AIN'T FIRST, YOU'RE LAST 140
CHAPTER 14: SHEDDING A TEAR FOR ALL TO SEE 142
CHAPTER 15: NOW THAT'S TRUST 145
CHAPTER 16: THIS IS LOYALTY 148
CHAPTER 17: NEVER GIVE UP 151
CHAPTER 18: AND THEN THERE WERE FOUR 155
CHAPTER 19: SECOND PLACE NEVER FELT SO GOOD 158

PART III: TALES FROM THE TRAILS 166
CHAPTER 20: SOLDIERS TO SUMMITS 167
CHAPTER 21: HAITI 173
CHAPTER 22: SUMMIT NIGHT 182
CHAPTER 23: IT'S NOT ABOUT THE MOUNTAIN 187
CHAPTER 24: SEEK THE FEAR, THEN POCKET IT 189
CHAPTER 25: SHERPAS 194
CHAPTER 26: STARBUCKS 197

CHAPTER 27: WILL THE REAL CIVILIZED CULTURE
PLEASE STAND UP? 202
CHAPTER 28: AVALANCHE OF LIFE 205
CHAPTER 29: THE WATER THAT BINDS 209
CHAPTER 30: SOMETIMES THE WRONG ROUTE TURNS
OUT TO BE THE RIGHT ROUTE.. 213
CHAPTER 31: MAKING FRIENDS WITH MY NEMESIS 220
CHAPTER 32: SOMETIMES A 60-FOOT BARRIER IS STRONGER
THAN WHAT'S INSIDE YOU.. 223

PART IV: EVEREST AIR... 228
CHAPTER 33: I WORK WITH SOME VERY BAD DUDES......... 230
CHAPTER 34: GO SAVE JESUS ON YOUR BIRTHDAY 234
CHAPTER 35: BE OF SERVICE TO YOUR OWN 238
CHAPTER 36: EVERYBODY GOES HOME 242

ABOUT THE AUTHOR 248
MORE ON JEFF EVANS AND MOUNTAIN VISION 250
ACKNOWLEDGEMENTS 252

**To all who seek out adventure
and find meaning within it.**

PREFACE

I wrote the first edition of *MountainVision: Lessons Beyond the Summit* when my son Jace was two years old. My career as an adventurer was firmly in place but my role as a writer was just as fresh and green as that of being a father. I had yet to discover the therapeutic effects writing about my experiences could have. Back then writing seemed laborious and felt like a dreaded high school chore. At some point, I had an epiphany that changed how I approached and perceived the act of adventure and theme-based writing. I began to appreciate the task of recounting the lessons I learned from each of my many subsequent global adventures. I began to find it an opportunity to revisit the powerful experiences that are present as we join teams and head out into the unknown.

For this edition, I wanted to maintain the autobiographical nature of the book but then add some of the select, "from-the-field" pieces that I have completed since the first edition. Part I stays true to the "how-I-got-here" content. Part II is a collection of my experiences on ABC's *Expedition Impossible,* where our team, *No Limits*, finished with a relatively proud second place. (I typically penned a recap of each of the episodes the day after the national airing on ABC.) In Part III you will find a collection of some of my most meaningful "field journals" with an effort to explore the meaningful messages that I discovered in my travels.

My son is now approaching his teen years and has read my book (which was somewhat of an enlightening experience for both of us). As I hope to continue exploring new adventurous opportunities in the future, I anticipate adding more material to Part III as the lessons continue to resonate with me.

I'm honored that you have chosen to spend some of your valuable time diving into my life and the lessons I have learned from living it.

Jeff Evans
Boulder, CO
February 2016

FOREWORD

I've spent over half of my life adventuring all over the globe: rock climbing, kayaking, mountaineering, adventure racing, and other ill-advised activities. Being blind, it has been a requisite that I share these adventures with partners and teammates. And as you can imagine, I am required to put every thread of trust into my partners. Every step, decision, and move I make requires a level of trust that most people will never begin to understand. I have to put my very life in the hands of my partners every step of each journey. I have had dozens of partners throughout my career but only one has been with me since the beginning. Most know him as Jeff. Those close to him call him Jefe. I call him my brother.

There's no doubt that Jeff and I have shared the highest and perhaps the lowest moments of our lives together. Every one of them, galvanizing the kind of friendship that only brothers can share. The kind of relationship that is based on suffering well together and caring deeply about the welfare of each other.

From our initial, naïve days together on the rocks in Joshua Tree, to the walls of El Capitan, to the summit of Mt. Everest, and well beyond, I can't even begin to imagine the countless hours the two of us have spent slogging up mountains, racing through river beds, mountain biking down steep trails, climbing vertical rock faces, and sleeping next to each other in stinky tents all over the world. We've cried, laughed and bled together on six of the seven continents.

Fast forward 20 plus years and I find it very satisfying to know that Jeff is able to share his message of servant leadership with audiences around the world, as I have always seen him as the consummate servant leader.

Whether it's through our decades of adventuring together or the countless other individuals I have watched him positively influence, he always seeks out ways to aid others in becoming a better version of themselves. Jeff chooses to give of himself. He chooses to be selfless. He chooses to nurture others.

What you will find in *MountainVision: Lessons Beyond the Summit* is a compilation of Jeff's rise from glorious "dirtbagdom" to a discovery of what it means to be a selfless leader. His writing style smoothly translates from his fluid personality.

Any of you that know him are quick to assess that Jeff is one of a kind. I can't imagine enjoying the "sufferfest" with anyone as much as I do with my brother, Jeff.

Now, enjoy the recounting of a remarkable life of adventure.

Erik Weihenmayer
Adventurer, Speaker, Author

Jeff in front of the north face of Everest.

PART I

CLIMBING MOUNTAINS

Life is such a curious process, full of wonder and excitement with countless opportunities to discover who we are and who we want to become. I feel very blessed to be able to travel the world with amazing individuals, all the while, gleaning pearls of knowledge and experience.

Part I of *MountainVision: Lessons Beyond the Summit* is a memoir of sorts. It is an abridged attempt to reflect on the road map that has led me to this curious place of self-discovery. I feel it's easy to walk your life path and incidentally look over the countless learning opportunities that are available at every turn. We should all challenge ourselves to be acutely conscientious and willing to reflect on what we are learning from each day and experience. With this knowledge, we are vastly more equipped to deal with all of life's summits and valleys.

Clinging desperately to the cascading wall of ice in front of me, I finally realize what the end looks like. I'm going to fall, and that will be that. My entire face goes numb and my heart screams as the rest of my body catches up with my inner ear.

A moment ago, I was clawing my way up this frozen tower. A split second later, one of my footholds breaks, and I'm sliding downward a half mile up. A million thoughts flood my mind, looking for a way—any way—out. My frenzied hands use ice picks to scratch against the slick surface in a losing fight. My boots find no new purchase; my legs flail wildly. I feel odd temperature extremes—the frozen ache of my ice-warped fingers and the white-hot burning of my face as the sun reflects off the mirror surface of the ice. The pain is intense and searing, but I can't stop fighting because I'm running out of time.

I know how this will end if I don't find a hold quickly. Only rocks lie thousands of feet below me, and the nearest hospital is hundreds of miles from here. There isn't a lot of doubt about what my fate would be.

A dozen yards lie between me and the drop that will send me to my death. *This is such a cliché, so many climbers I know have gone just like this...* Fifteen feet left now, still sliding ... *Why didn't I stay home?* Twelve feet ... *I don't want to die ...* Ten feet ... *I wish I'd called my mother ...* Five feet and I'm picking up speed ... *I wonder who will find my body?* My legs begin sliding out over the drop, swinging in the open air below them. Trees and bushes below look like small dots at this distance, but I'm aware of the jagged stones that surround them. I think of my family and hope they'll be alright.

And then, in that moment, I close my eyes. I'm cringing, holding my breath, and waiting, but the end doesn't come. Instead, I slowly open my eyes and realize that I'm stuck on something. I'm still lying face down on an icy ridge, my hands bruised to the bone, my face burnt and eyes blinded, but I'm breathing and not falling. There's nothing to do but smile and try to figure how long it will take me to get back up to where I was before I slipped.

MountainVision

Most people wonder from time to time how death will find them. For climbers this isn't just a morbid curiosity. Crawling up rocks and ice is one of those hobbies that provides you with plenty of opportunities to get whacked. I've got seconds to live, and a thought jumps into my head: *How does a guy who failed Racquetball end up here?*

I blame the ice cream man.

CHAPTER 1

NEVER LET GO

I'm asked again and again how I got started in climbing. It's tough to say how anyone truly gets into something like this, but I think it began when I was young. People like to imagine that I was the illegitimate child of a famous mountaineer and was raised by Sherpas. They wonder if I learned to walk on the icy slopes of Nepalese ranges, or maybe made my first ascents in the Alps while I was learning to read. These are good stories, but the truth is I grew up near the Blue Ridge Mountains in Virginia. If you were to look on a map or a globe, you'd notice that these mountains are marked with green, not white. Which is to say, they aren't very high. Most people think of my neck of the woods as a place where moonshine comes from, not adventurers.

My parents weren't globetrotting thrill seekers. Neither one of them has climbed anything higher than a ladder, never mind an enormous mass of ice and rock. My mom would have preferred that I take up chess or golf—both choices that would have made sense. Besides living about as far as one can from any major mountain ranges, I wasn't a standout physical specimen. I was deemed too small to play basketball, too weak to play football, and too slow to run track.

Despite all these strikes against me, I think it was inevitable that I found my way into the climbing lifestyle. Because even though I wasn't fast or strong, didn't come from the right place, and wasn't the descendent of a long line of adventurers, I always wanted to see more. I was always a *seeker*.

The great thing about being young is that it doesn't matter if you're too small or too slow—you don't know enough about life to be bothered by limitations. For a kid, an adventure might only be as far away as the front yard. And that's where the ice cream man comes in.

You see, when I was a small boy, maybe ten years old, the ice cream man was a magical and powerful figure. With a white truck, literally filled with ice cream, he was a minor deity in my eyes. He was also a very fast driver.

Jeff at three.

In those days, one of my favorite pastimes was to camp out in an old tree that grew in our yard. It had the kind of long, thick branches that just begged to be climbed. When school was out, I would spend those hot summer days scrambling from one wooden foothold to the next. For an imaginative kid, it was perfect. I would take in the breeze while sitting amongst the leaves, dreaming of faraway places. Those branches gave me a love of climbing and exploring that's never faded.

One of the few things that would get me out of that tree was the sound of the ice cream man coming. By the time the jingle-jangle music of his truck hit my ears, I knew there were only a few seconds to get down from the tree and flag him down. If I was too slow, he would pass my block and speed on to the next neighborhood, and I would go without ice cream. With so much at stake, I developed a habit of recklessly maneuvering down the tree and then sprinting out to the street. Every day, the truck's melody would reach me and I'd fly into action, my hands and feet knowing exactly where to go. I always took it for granted that the branches would hold me. And then the branches—like so many things we take for granted—let me down.

On one particularly hot afternoon, I was working my way down at the usual breakneck pace when one of the tree's small arms snapped beneath me. I held on above, but both my feet had given way, leaving me dangling high above the ground. I was too young to figure the distance to the ground, but familiar enough with casts and crutches to know I needed to keep holding on.

This is the first time that I can remember feeling like I'd worked myself into a spot I couldn't get out of. I struggled to think clearly, fighting back tears as the callous bark dug into my hands. It was frightening, but also exhilarating. At that moment, I was forced to learn an important lesson:
When you're stuck—in a tree, on a rock, or in life—you basically have two choices: fall, or find a way down.

With my fingers bleeding and my shoulders burning, I realized falling was not an option. I started to edge myself from side to side, trying to reach another branch. Each movement brought another wave of sharp pain. Every piece of me seemed to be begging to let go. But nothing hurt more than my hands. They stung and spilled fresh blood as I inched myself along the rough bark.

Finally, through short breaths and choked tears, I swung my left hand toward a smoother branch. If I could reach it, I'd make it to safety. But if I missed, I'd be in for a nasty spill. Luckily, I was able to get to it just in time, and after a couple more painful minutes, I was back down on the ground. The ice cream man was gone, but I had

MountainVision

discovered a passion and a strength that would help me for the rest of my life.

A strikingly similar situation has played itself out for me hundreds of times on rocks and ice around the world. The scenery changes—instead of being stranded in the branches of my favorite tree, I'm usually pitted against an unfriendly wall of rock and ice. But the premise is always the same: hang on or die.

Though sometimes the calls are a bit closer than I'd like them to be, I've survived in this profession not by being the biggest or fastest, but by choosing not to fall. You can choose to hang on, too. Remember, I'm just a kid who wanted some ice cream. Who were you?

CHAPTER 2

NEVER STOP SEEKING

By choosing not to fall for the first time, I had found some inner strength. But I still lacked discipline. Like a lot of kids with no direction, I did just enough to get by. I was that student who was always looking to squeak through with a barely passing grade. Outside the classroom, I was getting into minor trouble that landed me on the inside of a jail cell a couple of times. It was never anything serious, but anyone could see that I was just drifting through life without making a real effort.

I made my way to college at East Tennessee State, where I proceeded to set new lows for academic achievement. I was probably doomed from the start. When it came time to choose a major, I drew a blank. Part of me was drawn to medicine. As a child, my favorite toy had been a play medical kit that I'd gotten for my fifth birthday. I had carried it around with me for years, diagnosing friends and relatives, then "curing" them with the plastic stethoscope and hammer. Since then, medical work had been a dream of mine. But when I got to college, I found that my bad grades would almost certainly keep me from achieving that dream. Realizing how many years it would take to earn an MD didn't help, either.

With no other promising options, I decided on business. *After all*, I thought, *isn't that what most people study?*

MountainVision

Reasoning that almost everyone works in one business or another, I figured it would set me on the right path. Unfortunately, it didn't work out that way. I spent my days hanging out with friends and generally failing to show up for classes. After earning a stellar 1.25 GPA in my first semester, I was allowed back to school for a second try under academic probation.

I'd love to say that I'd learned my lesson and buckled down to graduate with honors. But I outdid my first effort by earning a 0.6 GPA in my second semester. In case your memory of the college grading scale is rusty, keep in mind that a student earns four points for an A, three for a B, and two for a C. They even give you a point for a D. So, to receive a cumulative grade of 0.6, you pretty much have to get a single D somewhere and then a bunch of F's. I didn't even pass Racquetball. In most states, this level of achievement doesn't simply disqualify a person from college, but also from being tried as an adult.

While my mental capabilities didn't classify me as handicapped, my motivation at that point probably could have. On the rare occasion that I'd actually go to class, I'd sleep through it and then go out drinking or hiking with my buddies. I just didn't understand what people saw in school, or why anyone should bother to pay attention. Today, someone with similar problems would probably be given a prescription for some kind of calming medicine, but at the time all I could do was find an outlet for my energy. And in climbing, I did. Just as that old tree had been my refuge when I was a small boy, the rock growths and wilderness areas near campus became a place for me to get away from the settings where I didn't fit in.

I had no patience for Biology or English, where everything felt so abstract and dull. It seemed pretty clear to me that the more I read, the more questions I'd have. And surely, more questions would only lead to more classes. In the classroom, there never seemed to be any action, only more words bouncing around and around—and no solid conclusions to be found. But on the side of a rocky hill, things were clear. All I had to do was concentrate and keep going up. Sooner or later, I'd reach the top.

After my grades came in for the second semester, continuing college was out of the question. With no sense of purpose, I decided it was time to go out and see something new. I wanted to get away from what I had already experienced and try my luck somewhere different. With $250 in my pocket, I decided to go where anyone who had a passion for climbing would—Colorado. I expected a stiff lecture from my parents, but to their credit, they didn't try to keep me from it. I think they realized that sending me back to school was pointless. Perhaps they thought I'd come back home after being out in the world for a couple of months. Maybe they figured I'd be broke and hungry, but also ready to buckle down and grow up. What they didn't realize was that I wasn't interested in money or a good job. I wanted to find something that would pull me out of bed each morning and bring some adventure to my life.

The drive out west was long, but I loved every minute of it. As the green hills in the Southeast gave way to the wide-open plains across Kansas and Oklahoma, my mind raced with the new possibilities in front of me. Eventually, I could see the mountains towering in the distance, like heavy thunderclouds all the way up into the sky. Once I reached the Rockies, I was in love. These were the kinds of rugged hills I'd always dreamed of, places where you could explore for weeks and never find yourself on the same trail.

When I stopped driving, I found myself in a small Colorado mountain town. I began working odd jobs as a dishwasher or bellboy, barely keeping myself fed. The rest of the time, I poured my energy into climbing. Every day was a chance to explore a new rock or meet a new summit. My hair grew long and I scraped my fingers every day until they bled. My climbing mind grew sharp. I kept this up for a couple of years, until I decided I needed some new scenery and headed west to Joshua Tree in California.

MountainVision

If you aren't a climber, Joshua Tree is probably what you'd think of as a wasteland. A couple hours east of Los Angeles, it's basically a desert with some very mystical rock structures jutting from the earth. Inside the park, formations fill the landscape for as far as the eye can see in any direction. Some are small, only 20 or 30 feet up on a side. Others are larger, like apartment buildings, with walls that curve and shift at extreme angles.

By the time I arrived, I was what climbing enthusiasts might call a rock rat. Normal people might have called me a dirtbag. I was taking poverty and lack of motivation to a whole new level. In Colorado, I'd lived in basements for a few dollars a week. Now I decided to give up those luxuries so I wouldn't have to hold a job. I didn't have any steady income, but I was completely unencumbered. I still needed a few dollars here and there to get by, but otherwise I was free to do whatever I wanted. Sleeping in the back of a pickup truck without regular, gainful employment isn't what most folks consider a worthy endeavor, but for me it was the best thing in the world. I spent my days doing the only thing I cared about—climbing. Other activities, such as scrounging for food or taking the occasional day job to buy new gear, were aimed at getting me back to climbing.

Some kids graduate from college, some go straight into the military or the workforce, a few even backpack around Europe for a while. Not me. I decided to give the homeless route a try. And while most people would consider this a waste of time, it was the best thing that could have happened to me. I was finally free of the hopes and expectations everyone else had for me. In that space, I was able to discover what motivation and focus were really about. Instead of doing things for other people, or because I was supposed to, I started thinking for myself. I didn't want to be a lawyer or an accountant, but I probably didn't want to live outside forever, either. I finally started taking a look at my future and realizing I could follow things that would make me happy—although I wasn't totally sure what that meant.

I hadn't given much thought to going back to school, though I wasn't completely against the idea. The issue was that I still didn't see how academic study could take me anywhere I wanted to go. The rest of the world might think college was a good idea, but I felt like I'd been there and done that. Still, you can only escape the rest of the world for so long.

There were a lot of parties in Joshua Tree, but they weren't formal, catered affairs. Usually, someone from the "community" scraped together a few dollars for pizza and beer, along with whatever else they might be growing in the desert. People crawled out of vans, tents, or trucks and got together to celebrate being dirtbag hippies. These get-togethers were a great time, but they didn't lead to a lot of interaction with the outside world. I grew to occasionally miss things like clean towels, food that didn't come in bar form, and, especially, girls who didn't smell like they'd been climbing in the desert heat for three weeks straight. So, when one of my friends invited me to a party outside the park, I jumped at the chance. And there, I met a girl who would change my life.

To write in a book that a chance meeting with a pretty girl changed your life is a bit cliché, but it's true nonetheless. What's unusual about my story is that this girl didn't end up being a significant figure in my life. It was only one moment—a single conversation—that changed my course. I was having a great time that evening, taking in the fresh smells and sights, when I saw her. She caught my eye right away, pulling me out of whatever thoughts were swimming around in my head. She was tall and beautiful, but it wasn't her physical attractiveness that struck me right away. It was the way she seemed to radiate confidence and poise. Even from a distance, I could see she spoke evenly, with a measured tone. She thought for a moment before she spoke, and everyone seemed to listen. Not only because she was stunning, but also because she had interesting thoughts and ideas.

Approaching her wouldn't be easy. To say that she was outside my normal circle of friends is a bit of an understatement. I looked and smelled like a refugee, while every detail of her appearance seemed to suggest a kind of purpose and precision. Despite our differences, I knew I had to try.

MountainVision

I walked over and gave my best opening pitch, trying to gently work my way into the conversation at hand. Probably sensing my interest, or possibly my lack of deodorant, her friends peeled away from us one by one. I kept the conversation moving with questions about her life: where she was from, what she liked to do—all the while doing my best to pretend to know about and like those things.

Talking with her was fascinating and intimidating. I found out she was a student at Brown University, in the Ivy League, and nearing her graduation. She had been to places I hadn't seen, read books I'd never heard of, and quoted people whose names I couldn't pronounce. By the end of the evening, I had figured out two things: she wasn't interested in coming back to my sleeping bag in the park, and I wanted to be more like her. I knew I was never going to get there without going back to school.

But this realization brought its own problems. It had been years since I'd picked up a book. And with my poor track record, what college would accept me? On top of all this, I still didn't know what I wanted to study.

I spent the next few days thinking these things over. majors that got I knew I wanted to learn about different people around the world. Finally, it hit me like a two-ton artifact—cultural anthropology. Maybe I could use my actual interests to propel me forward, instead of shrinking back and ignoring my real motivation.

To pursue my new plan, I knew I needed to get out of Joshua Tree. I continued living in my truck to save money, but I took a part-time job at a local climbing gear outfitter. I began stashing the earnings from my tiny paychecks until I could move into a real place again. After a few months, I'd saved enough and decided I would go back to Colorado.

In a small alpine village, I found a mobile home with a rent that cost me next to nothing. I used the rest of my money to begin taking some correspondence classes. When I came to "previous college" on the application, I simply checked "none." As the weeks went by, I devoured the lessons that arrived by mail. Week after week, I worked with books, quizzes, and papers, flying through one course and then another. I found I actually loved learning, and began to regret the years I'd spent away from it. All the while I was terrified the university might find out about my previous stint and revoke my admission, but the expulsion never came.

I buried myself in my studies with the same focus I'd previously reserved for climbing. But I didn't want to give up my love of the outdoors. My parents, wanting to help me make something of myself, pitched in. Despite their help, it became clear that I could no longer afford to skip work and go out climbing every day if I wanted to keep paying my rent and tuition.

The decision to almost completely give up my one true love for another pursuit was heart wrenching for me. I worked in kitchens or hotels, taking small jobs in the industries that spring up around ski towns. I'd stumble through my duties, wishing I were in the hills climbing, instead of scraping food from dishes or carrying luggage. On my few days off from work and studying, I'd head to a local rock face and climb from dawn to dusk.

This might have gone on for months or years if I hadn't run into some new climbers one morning. The sun was just breaking out, and I wanted to get up the rock wall I was working on one more time before I had to shuttle off to work. The group saw me climbing from below and was impressed by the comfort I showed while moving across the face. New to the sport, they would slowly amble their way towards the top, double checking each hold, tentatively working with their ropes and gear. For someone like me who had gone through years of daily climbing, the section was nearly effortless. Just as an experienced ballplayer might step out to the batting cages to relieve stress, I was on this pitch for the relaxation, not the challenge. Noticing the vast difference in our skill, one of these climbers approached me about an impromptu lesson. I said I'd love to help out, but that I needed to get back to work to pay the rent. "Maybe some other time," I told them. And then, I reached another pivotal moment in my life. A member of the group offered to pay me for my time.

MountainVision

I had heard of guiding for money, but never thought it was something I could do. I didn't work for any big company or have any special training. I was just a climbing bum who had learned some things. I didn't consider myself to be any kind of expert, but that didn't matter. What I learned that day was, if you have a lot more knowledge and experience on a topic than someone else, to that person you're an expert. You can help them get to where they want to go, even if you're still working out your own challenges on a different level. This turned out to be a life revelation that would take me far.

In the following weeks, I took on more and more guiding clients. I didn't want to work for a big company or wear a tie, but best of all this gave me a reason to be out in the mountains when I wasn't studying. I made a point of being out where other climbers would be around. Newer climbers would see me scaling the rocks and ask if I'd take them up or show them some tips. So, I started charging a few dollars for an on-the-spot lesson. Soon, I was giving longer lessons, and then leading overnight trips on actual mountains. Eventually, I was able to quit the other odd jobs I worked. I was barely earning enough money to pay the bills, but more importantly, I was learning to be responsible for other people. In the end, that new sense of responsibility made the rest of my life—and the stories that make up the rest of this book—possible.

After completing a few correspondence classes, I moved on to a full-time program at the University of Colorado. I spent the next three years trying to make my way by keeping up a schedule that would allow me to make academic progress, live indoors, and keep climbing. I would sign up for morning classes so that I could guide climbers in hills near campus during the afternoon. I'd then shuttle back home in the evening to study.

It was a great life, and it gave me a good outlet for all of my energy and ambition. Just as I'd learned I could enjoy my education, I came to discover I appreciated guiding as well. What I had first pursued for the money was turning out to give me deeper fulfillment. There was something amazing about working with my clients to make them stronger, better climbers. Many of them became interested in climbing because they had seen others scaling rocks and wanted to try the sport themselves. Often, however, they lacked the confidence to learn, and would start out afraid and doubting themselves. Hour by hour, as their technical skills improved, I watched their hesitation melt away. Seeing the sense of accomplishment in their faces and watching fear turn into strength began to seem more valuable than the few dollars that were exchanged for my services.

What's more, this newfound fulfillment carried over into my coursework. My grades were better than they had ever been, even after I began taking extra classes to finish my degree more quickly. My only real question was what to do after graduation. I loved my studies in anthropology, but I couldn't find anything in the field that would keep me outdoors, and I knew I wouldn't function well in an office environment. Luckily, the answer found me.

Jeff standing on top of the first Flatiron in Boulder, CO.

I woke up early one Saturday morning, reveling in the freedom and possibilities promised by a morning without classes or clients. I decided to head to the outskirts of town to scale the Boulder Flatirons. The Flatirons are a set of massive stone walls that jump out at you from miles away. The array of jagged faces, all of them nearly vertical, make the small mountain that they sit upon look as if it had been carved open on its side. Like the Diamond, the Flatirons have a geometry that makes them beautiful to hikers and irresistible to climbers. They were also a convenient choice, requiring only a short drive and a few hours to complete.

I had scaled the Flatirons dozens, if not hundreds of times, so I let my thoughts wander as I set out on the short trail that led to the first pitch. While my mind wrestled with all of my worries about the future, turning the possibilities over and over, I trod through the high grass and rough thickets of the springtime Colorado backcountry. I was so lost in my own thoughts that I didn't notice the pieces of gear glinting and reflecting just off the gravel path until I was only a few yards away.

I leaned over for a closer look, examining small shards of shiny metal and bright fabric strewn across the green and brown surface. Slowly, I edged my way into the brush, already sure and afraid of what I would find. A few steps in and I saw more scraps, and a large impression in the earth no more than three yards farther. I couldn't see into the smothered, depressed bushes, but there was no longer any doubt. Bears didn't wear bright orange. I reached out my hand to clear away the small twigs and gazed upon the fallen climber.

I prayed silently that he would be alive and well, but he wasn't making a sound. It was possible, I reasoned, that he might just be injured. Either way, I didn't know what to do. I studied him for a moment, limp and unmoving, and then began to yell for help. My voice carried through to the trail, and soon half a dozen others had joined me, all of us screaming out for someone who could help.

Now I could see that the fallen climber was taking short breaths, but I still wasn't sure how to help. The only thing that came to mind was to keep clamoring, and so I did. After a few minutes of this, a man came rushing down the path and pushed people aside to reach the fallen climber. He moved in toward the body quickly, but with precision. He used a finger to check the man's pulse and lowered his ear to listen for breathing. His hands moved with practiced skill, calm in spite of the panic around him. He began to check the fallen man for breaks and bruises, and then spent time reviving his patient. Finally, he rose, stepped away from the climber, and informed us the young man would be alright. The climber had shattered an ankle and had the wind knocked out of him, but the injuries were much less serious than they could have been.

In that moment, my mind was flooded by those old dreams of medicine going all the way back to my childhood. The thought of so many years of school still seemed overwhelming, but I wanted to be a doctor just like this man. I overcame the shock of the last few minutes to walk with him as the injured climber was carried to get further medical attention. I wanted to find out where he worked, where he'd gone to medical school, and how I could learn the skills he had. His expression was one of slight surprise and amusement. "Oh, I'm not a doctor," he explained. "I'm an EMT."

I went straight home to find out whatever I could about Emergency Medical Technicians. I found out that EMT's were often the first line of medical care, especially in the backcountry. There was even a unique kind of tech, the Wilderness EMT, who specialized in situations like the one I'd seen. Courses were three months long, and available in Colorado. I began to think, trying to conjure up ways to afford the tuition. One course began just days after my graduation, not leaving me much time to save. I couldn't find a way, but my mind wouldn't let it go. I had finally found a track that would allow me to combine my love of medicine and my love of mountains. I couldn't bear the thought of not pursuing it.

As luck would have it, the perfect opportunity arrived. My parents, proud and relieved that I'd given up homelessness to work my way to a college degree, wanted to get me something special for graduation. They asked what it was that I was dying to have. Was it a car, a new computer, maybe a vacation abroad? I think they were stunned when I told them I wanted tuition for another course. Like a five-year-old in the supermarket check-out line with a small toy in hand, I proceeded to list off all of the wonderful benefits I could get from the program, and how it wasn't that expensive at all if you really thought about it. It was an investment in my future, and I'd certainly learn skills that would carry over to a lucrative position. On and on I went, until they finally stopped me mid-sentence. They would cover my tuition. They were just happy I didn't ask for a holiday in Amsterdam.

The Wilderness EMT course was a blast. I learned about basic life support, wound care and other forms of medical treatment, and the ins and outs of backcountry medical emergencies. I also made close friends. Suddenly, I found myself in a community of men and women who understood me. The people who sign up for a course like this do so because they want to help others, but also because they love wild places. The people I met could relate to the restlessness I felt in the classroom or an office. Like me, they'd decided they wanted lives filled with adventure—but not without the occasional shower or hot meal. The weeks went by like a dream. Mornings were filled with practical, hands-on medical training, usually outdoors. Our afternoons were free for climbing, kayaking, and talking about the techniques we'd learned that day.

It was during the first week of class that I met Sam, a fellow climber and student. He was in his twenties, just like I was, and also looking for a way to make more out of his love for the backcountry. He was newer to climbing but shared my love of adventure. He would try anything.

He'd been skydiving, windsurfing, and hiking through some of the most rugged terrain in the state. He was new to technical climbing, but was absorbing it passionately and with the same abandon. He took in new rocks and hills every week, going up with anyone who was interested. In his hometown of Phoenix, he had even gone climbing with a friend of his who was blind. I couldn't

Lizard Head, Colorado

imagine such a thing. Sam and I hit it off right away, and would often spend time studying or climbing together. One Friday morning, just after classes, he asked if I'd be interested in taking in a longer technical climb over the weekend. With no plans in place, it seemed like a great idea.

We decided we would climb Lizard Head, a moderately difficult hunk of jagged stone, cut out from the earth deep in the San Juan range of the Rocky Mountains. While not as high or technically challenging as many climbs in the Rockies, Lizard Head can be tough because it wears you down. Just reaching the base of the rock from the trailhead requires a hike of about a day. Then, the ascent itself is a climb that can take more than eight hours. During the climb, you only scale about 800 vertical feet. But your starting point is 12,000 feet above sea level, and the path you must follow twists and bends around craggy features. Plus, the lack of oxygen at that starting altitude makes the ascent physically demanding. Add the unpredictable weather and the remote location, and you've got a tough haul with very little chance for help if you need it.

Our approach hike was long and grueling, the path leading to the face marked by worn trails that had often turned to scree, piles of small pebbles that easily give way under foot. Relishing the challenge, we kept a steady pace on a path that crept first through a dense, forested corridor, and then twisted and turned into nothing more than ashen gray rocks above tree line. There was no way through except to keep putting one foot after another, which we did until the vertical rope climb leading to the top was in sight. Here, we set up camp for the evening. Sam and I settled in, eager to go the rest of the way. We didn't have to wait too long.

In the early hours of the morning, our alarm went off and we set out toward the top. For several hours we clawed our way up, inch by inch, conquering each of the thousand feet in small sips of breath and pain. We finally reached the summit, exhausted, but pleased to have made it. We sat together, taking in the silence and peace of the moment. I crouched on the ground and lay back to catch my breath and take in the afternoon sun. Sam pulled out his camera to snap a few photos, and thus became the first one to spot the nasty weather brewing on the horizon.

Discerning the difference between good and bad weather in the mountains can be a bit of a guessing game, as mountain clouds are notoriously ambiguous, but this wasn't one of those times. The puffy, gray clouds approaching the summit were unmistakable. In our enjoyment of a hard route, we hadn't noticed that the day was reaching late into the afternoon—prime time for mountain storms.

In other words, we had reached the summit just in time for the meteorological equivalent of rush-hour traffic.

Our satisfaction melted into fear as we started to calculate the time it would take us to descend against the number of precious minutes left before the weather would arrive. Our only option was to hurry back down the rocky tower we were still exhausted from climbing. With no more time to enjoy the summit and take in the views, we started down.

Moving quickly but not recklessly, we hoped the thunder we could hear in the distance would hold off just long enough. After about twenty minutes of frenzied movement, dodging sharp edges with tired legs and bleary eyes, we realized that we weren't going to reach the safety of camp in time. Perched on a small, flat stone, I sat with my legs folded to my chest to keep them from dangling over the side of a cliff that went down at least seven stories. We were in the thick of it, with the sky rumbling above us, another three or four rope-lengths of descent lying below. There was no easy way out.

I wasn't sure what to do. The descent would be dangerous, but trying to wait out the storm on a tiny ledge might kill us. When you're loaded down with climbing gear—thousands of pieces of jangling metal—a thunderstorm is not something you want to be caught in. The wind was picking up and small pebbles stung my eyes. I knew we couldn't stay long. A loud clap of thunder came with a flash of lightning not far enough away, and the hairs on the back of my neck told me they understood the trouble. My nerves were starting to eat me alive, but just like when I was stuck in the tree as a boy, I realized we had a choice: we could either lose our cool and, almost certainly, our lives, or stay calm and keep working our way toward the bottom. I decided that if I was going to die, I'd rather have it be on the way down.

Sam had apparently arrived at the same conclusion but seemed to be dealing with it differently. As the seriousness of our trouble set in, he started talking more quickly and desperately.

"I don't want to get pasted here," he murmured.

MountainVision

I told him we should try to make our way down a bit farther. We took a glance over the ledge, where we would use our gear and ropes to try a descent, when I realized Sam was on the verge of losing his head.

Fear is a natural emotion, and it has its place in any adventure. After all, without the sense of fear and risk, climbs would become nature walks and wouldn't carry the excitement they do. But Sam's fear had overcome him. He was becoming unhinged, and it was making our situation even more dangerous. Because my climbing experience gave me a keen awareness of how dire things were, I was probably more afraid than he was. But I knew we needed to manage our fear and move on if we were to have any hope of surviving.

So, in a gesture fit for Hollywood, I slapped Sam across the face and told him to pull it together. I explained that if we were going to be killed, a quick fall would be better than waiting there to be blown off the cliff or struck by lightning. Sam didn't speak, but he nodded in agreement and we started to move down.

The rocks were smooth and worn, there was nowhere to grip or place any equipment. Our only option was an old rappel point that had been left behind by a previous team. I didn't like the looks of it. The small anchor that would hold our weight was nothing more than a piton, a tiny tool, resembling a small spike, which can be driven into loose rock. As I inserted the rope, the piton flexed and gave way. I couldn't be sure if it would hold our weight, but we didn't have any other options.

I headed down on the first rappel. The wet rocks conspired with a biting wind to swing us from side to side as the anchor swiveled. I expected it to pop out at any moment, dropping us backward to the ground below. I felt petrified of the fall, but each time I came close to stopping, I would look up at the hard rain and lightning crashing up at the peak and find the courage to make my way a bit farther down.

Of course, we eventually made it to the bottom with a few new scars and a story to tell. Sam had composed himself beautifully and even went first on several of the rappels when I became too fatigued.

Down at the base, he acknowledged he had lost his nerve for a moment and needed that slap to bring him back.

Moments like those are not uncommon between climbing buddies, and it wouldn't have been a big deal if Sam hadn't mentioned again his friend, Erik, the blind climber. After what we'd been through that day, he thought I should give working with Erik some more thought. Erik was a good friend, Sam told me, and someone who was ready to take his adventuring to the next level. But, he wouldn't be able to do it alone. Sam said there was no one else with whom he'd rather trust his friend and that we might make a good team. I told him I would think about it, and for the first time, I actually did.

CHAPTER 3

THE RIGHT FIT

When I first met Erik Weihenmayer, I was living in Joshua Tree again. After the years of hard work spent getting first my degree and then my wilderness EMT certification, I wanted to blow off some steam. The manager of a local gear company with whom I'd kept in touch had offered me the chance to work selling climbing equipment. It would only be a few hours for the remainder of the summer, but it sounded like the perfect chance to regroup and get back to my dirtbag climbing roots.

I'd bought an old pickup truck for the trip west and made it my home for the next few months. Each week I worked a couple of shifts at the store so I could afford ramen noodles and the occasional beer. When I wasn't working, I climbed all day until it was time to crawl back into my sleeping bag and wait for the next morning. Sometimes I didn't shower for weeks on end, which meant I usually woke up smelling like sweaty garbage. And I was loving all of it.

For everything I'd accomplished, I came to realize that sometimes it feels good to just let go and live carefree. Some people save for vacations to Paris or Tahiti, but I just wanted to get back to the desert.

Erik "Super Blind" Weihenmayer

I had given some thought to what Sam had said back in Colorado, and decided I would give it a shot. I got in touch with Erik and asked if he wanted to come on out to my "home." He said he'd love to. Joshua Tree would serve as a good barometer of Erik's talents and abilities, and I figured it would give us a chance to see what kind of climbing chemistry we had.

When Sam's car pulled up, I saw Erik for the first time. Sam helped him from the car, while I looked on in disbelief from the bed of my truck. Forget about mountains or cliff faces—I couldn't imagine that this guy could make it up the stairs. He looked like a mess in every conceivable way. He was obviously athletic, but was so white that I wondered if he might have gone blind from living in a cave. His pale skin was accentuated by an outfit that made him look like a roadie for the world's most awkward metal band. He sported a mullet, tattered jeans, a t-shirt, and a denim jacket with an Iron Maiden patch on it. Worst of all, the different kinds of denim didn't even seem to go together. Neither did his socks. I wondered if there was some sort of blind-dressing-the-blind thing going on. *Wow*, I thought, *he's not just blind—he's colorblind!*

I was already a bit skeptical, but after Sam introduced us, the ridiculousness of the situation became apparent. Here I was, essentially homeless, surrounded by desert and rocks, and preparing to lead a blind man—complete with dog and stick—on a climbing expedition. For his part, Erik seemed to either sense my lack of enthusiasm, or was having doubts of his own.

I knew he couldn't see me, but I still tried to hide the skepticism from my face. The moment was heavy and awkward. No one said anything. Finally, I mumbled that we might as well go up some rocks while the day was young. I thought it best to get this over with as quickly as possible. I resigned myself to a ruined morning, but thought I might still be able to get rid of Erik by afternoon. And so, with the help of his seeing-eye dog, I led the way over to the first pitch.

The Joshua Tree dirtbags were used to seeing a lot of things. Plenty of situations that might seem outrageous in the civilized world wouldn't cause them to look twice. This was a place that attracted people who wanted to live in trucks and vans and crawl around dusty rocks all day. Drunken fights, bad acid trips, and naked climbers were all ordinary occurrences. Now I had something that topped them all. As my neighbors peered on curiously, I led the way for a man with a seeing-eye dog to the first pitch and roped him up. Jaws dropped. I could see men and women looking at one another and mouthing "Are you serious?" to one another. We were about to find out.

I started up the first pitch. It was a relatively easy climb, and one I'd done several times before. I moved from hold to hold quickly and smoothly, hoping to expedite Erik's departure back to wherever he'd come from. I couldn't remember what I'd been thinking when I agreed to this, but both lobes of my brain now considered it a mistake. Clearly, the thing to do was to get to the top and let him figure out why there were no other blind climbers.

I reached the end of the short pitch quickly. Now it was Erik's turn. Without any hesitation, he reached up to find the first hold and then the second. He wasn't fast, but he wasn't sloppy either. He seemed to have a natural sense for positioning, and would slip easily from one spot to the next. I wondered if I'd underestimated him. He might even be able to enjoy himself on some of the easier sections while I kept an eye out. Before long, he reached the top where I was waiting. I was impressed with his grit, and thought about taking him somewhere more challenging after he'd had a chance to rest and catch his breath. But before either of us could get comfortable, he turned to me and asked, "What's next?" I couldn't help but smile.

Curious now, I led him down and onto a more difficult route, this one longer and more technically challenging. Again, he surprised me with his calm determination. While he didn't have the benefit of experience, he never got flustered and simply kept moving until he found his way. He was a very strong climber for a beginner, sighted or otherwise. In fact, getting up the pitches wasn't the hard part for him. Rather, it was getting from one rock to the next. The park was crowded with people and gear, which Erik occasionally walked into or through.

He, of course, couldn't see anybody, and no one seemed to be looking out for him. Several times, as we made our way from one formation to another, he'd crash into another group of climbers. I tried to steer him with the help of his dog, but it was impossible to stop him from getting in the way. He never complained or said he was sorry, just made his way through until we were ready to start a new pitch. He seemed to understand that people just didn't expect to see a blind man climbing in Joshua Tree, but he didn't apologize for it either.

Following each ascent, I'd look at him, pale and mulleted in his mismatched clothes. I had worried he wouldn't have the stamina to make it up even one stone face. Instead, he took climb after climb, never slowing down or asking for rest.

After a few hours, we became familiar enough for me to ask the questions that had been on my mind all day. Who was this guy and why was he doing this?

Erik's dad was a retired Marine. Like a lot of military children, he had grown up in different places all around the world. His early years in Shanghai, Korea, Europe, and throughout the U.S. had instilled in him a strong sense of adventure and curiosity. He couldn't see, but he always wanted to know how new things sounded, smelled, and, especially, felt.

Erik hadn't been born blind. As a child he had been diagnosed with retinoschisis, a degenerative eye disease that caused his retina to unravel over time. The condition was irreversible, and from a very early age he knew that he would eventually go completely blind. His sight continued to worsen, growing darker and darker until, by his tenth birthday, he could barely make out shapes and faces.

He was completely robbed of his sight by age thirteen. That same year his mother was traumatically killed in a car accident. For many children, these losses would have been crippling, but they left Erik only tougher and more resilient. Erik's father continued to impress upon his three sons the importance of family, pulling the boys even closer to him and each other. To the outside world, Erik's father and brothers were fiercely protective of the youngest family member. But they didn't allow him to use his blindness as an excuse to stop achieving in his life.

And Erik had not only achieved, but also flourished. Academically, he excelled, earning a master's degree in education from Boston University. He had landed a very prestigious teaching assignment at the Phoenix Country Day School. He had also continued his family's adventurous tradition, taking on long hikes in central Asia with the help of guides.

His first climbing lessons came early. As a teenager, he had attended a camp for the blind. The camp had a 20-foot wall that could be scaled. He made his way up the wall again and again, dozens of times in an afternoon, finding and testing different ways up its constructed face. Long after the other campers had moved on to other activities, he found himself experimenting with holds and movements. It wasn't much of a start, but it had given him an early love of climbing that he hadn't forgotten in the years since.

When he moved to Phoenix, he decided that he wanted to push his love for climbing further. The problem was, nobody else wanted to go along for the ride. He joined rock-climbing gyms and had good conversations with the other members. But when he tried to generate interest in an actual outdoor climb, people always seemed to be unavailable.

He tried hanging out near the rock gardens that dot the Arizona countryside, having close friends help him find his way up the sharp, red stones. Other people were consistently impressed with his skill. But again, when it came time to talk about meeting somewhere for a longer ascent, the whole world seemed to have a dentist appointment that day. Despite the admiration, it seemed clear that nobody wanted to get stuck dragging him around, or worse, explaining the situation if he got hurt.

In desperation, he started calling established guides. Since he couldn't find partners the way other climbers did, he was prepared to pay someone to teach him. But this didn't work out either. Once the guides got word of his condition, their calendars filled up. It seemed that he was never going to find anyone who would train with him until he met Sam, a fellow teacher at the Phoenix Country Day School. Sam's open mind and carefree attitude made him an ideal partner and friend. The two of them spent hours at the rock gym and outside on short pitches learning the fundamentals together. Now, though, he wanted to do something bigger and he needed a technically stronger partner.

I was starting to think that maybe Erik wasn't just a charity case. For a new climber, he was strong, and no one could question his heart. We did dozens of ascents that first afternoon, each time trying a different feature that would challenge Erik in a new way. He sometimes paused, but never showed frustration or anger. He simply examined a problem and then dealt with it.

Near dusk, I was so impressed with his attitude that I decided to take him up one last pitch. This would be the longest and hardest so far. It was a roughly shaped spire that crawled and cragged its way up over 600 feet, at times forcing the climber to move, hanging and inverted, up a concave surface. Think of trying to climb up your living room wall and then across the ceiling and you've got a sense of the climb. This pitch could be a challenge for even an experienced rock rat, much less a rookie who'd been working hard since morning.

I forged up the side, feeling the effects of the day's work myself. Erik followed steadily, never moving too quickly, nor falling behind. At times he would reach out, searching for the next hold. I started to provide small verbal directions. I never told him exactly where to move. Rather, I gave him general instructions, allowing him to figure out the final solutions for himself. He never asked for more than he needed and he never became overwhelmed when the route was arduous. He just kept attacking, slowly and methodically. It was an impressive display. At times I forgot that he couldn't see where he was going.

At last we reached the top of the rock, and sat for a rest on a smooth, flat stone. The sun was retiring, and my muscles ached. I had been impressed enough by Erik's climbing to think I actually wanted to go out and try it with him again sometime. I gave him the good news, but his answer was short and impatient.

"That's great, but what are we going to do now?"

I was a bit confused. "Well, I suppose we should get down and have some dinner."

"Let's climb some more."

"Erik," I said, "it's been a long day. I'm tired. Plus, it's getting dark." I lifted my leg to pick some of the pebbles out of my shoes. "Look, let's get some sleep. I'll take you again in the morning."

"You can be tired tomorrow. Do you think I care if it's dark?"

I looked up at him. He wasn't kidding. He just stood there, waiting for me to come up with the next excuse so that he could convince me to keep going. At that moment, I finally began to understand what climbing was to him. It wasn't just about doing something different. This wasn't going to be a hobby for him. He was out climbing because he had to, and this was the chance that he'd waited months for. Erik wasn't adventurous—he was a lunatic. He was just like me.

CHAPTER 4

TRAINING WHEELS

Even after climbing with Erik that weekend, I wasn't convinced that taking him up a real mountain would be a good idea. More accurately, others convinced me. In my excitement, I told some of my friends and family about what we'd done, and about the chance that we could do something great together. They didn't share my enthusiasm. Instead, they were shocked to learn that I'd gone climbing with a blind man.

"What the hell were you thinking?" one of my closest friends demanded.

He wasn't alone. While some were more diplomatic, everyone thought it was a bad idea. Didn't I know he could get hurt? What was I trying to prove? Why couldn't I find a sighted partner?

Doubt crept in, and I started to think they might be right. Still, I couldn't forget how Erik and I had bonded that weekend. I genuinely enjoyed climbing with him and truly felt he had the kind of strength and inner fire I could rely on in a tough situation. Without me, I wondered if he would ever get his chance to do some real mountaineering. I had seemed to be his best prospect so far, and it had taken him several months and a drive to California just to find someone who would even spend an afternoon rock climbing with him. He deserved a chance.

Jeff Evans

Before he left Joshua Tree we'd had a conversation about taking this further. Could I work with him, he wanted to know, or would I be too afraid?

My answer was truthful, but noncommittal. I told him I thought he was an unusually strong climber, and that anyone would be lucky to go climbing with him. It was the climbing equivalent of taking a number at the end of the night and promising to call. We both knew I might not get in touch with him, that I might decide I was also too busy to climbing with a blind man.

Erik didn't wait for my call. He got in touch with me by calling the store where I worked. He said he was coming through California the next week and wanted to get together for a drink. I wasn't sure I wanted to, but I didn't have a lot of choice. One of the downsides to being homeless is that you can't really say you're too busy to see someone. There was no way he was going to believe that I had other plans, so we set a time to meet.

As Erik's visit sat on the back of my mind, I went about introducing myself into the civilized world. I was looking for employment that would take me through the rest of the year, and decided to visit a friend at Berkeley while I checked out some prospective jobs in the area. While I was in town, he asked me if I wanted to go with him and hear a public speaker. I didn't have any plans, so I decided to tag along. Neither of us was that interested in business, but we went, mostly because it was free and there were complimentary snacks.

The speaker was John Scully, former President of Pepsi, and then CEO of Apple. I had never heard someone talk about business in a way that didn't relate to numbers and dry statistics. In his speech came what I will always think of as my epiphany moment. In a section about planning, he said "The future belongs to those who see the possibilities before they become obvious." I had never heard something so simple and so profound. I grabbed a pen from another audience member who was busy scribbling notes. I was so afraid I would forget this seemingly powerful statement; I wrote it on my hand. Even now, I'm amazed at how that phrase seemed to fit in with where I was in my life and guide me in the right direction.

Later that week, I met Erik at a small dive bar in Joshua Tree. After a couple of beers and small talk about his students, he got down to business. He wanted to do a mountain. Not a hill, not a rock formation, not a daytrip up a small face. He wanted a real alpine experience. He'd come to find out if I would be in for such a trip.

I didn't have to think about it. I already knew what he'd come for. His unrelenting pursuit of this goal—the same stubborn determination that had caused him to come to California in the first place and to return uninvited—wouldn't have allowed for anything else. If I didn't agree, he might drive back dozens or even hundreds of times until I did.

I told Erik to count me in, but I didn't just want to do a climb. I wanted to do something big. He leaned in. If we were going to do this, I told him, I wanted it to be about more than just getting up some rock. I wanted us to do something extraordinary together.

"Let's not just create a goal," I blurted out. "Let's make a ... *vision.*" The word seemed to hang in the air. *Had I just told a blind man I wanted to create a vision?* The thought, coupled with the beers, made me start to giggle. I bit my lip and tried to stay silent. I wondered if he could hear me trying not to laugh. What would that sound like, and would he know the sound?

Erik leaned back and seemed to take this in. I couldn't tell if he was thinking about what I'd said, or was insulted by my insensitivity. After a moment he leaned forward. I waited anxiously for his words, but before he could speak he just broke into laughter. Leaning forward and grabbing his stomach through heavy chuckles, the only word I could make out was 'vision,' followed by more laughter.

When we finally stopped laughing, we started thinking about a specific goal that we would work toward. Even more than his climbing talent, I loved that Erik seemed to understand what I meant right away. The difference between a goal and a vision might seem slight, but it couldn't be more important.

Jeff Evans

Vision, the thing that you conceive or imagine, doesn't have anything to do with your eyes. It's bigger than that. It's your sense of the world and what could be possible, even if it doesn't seem so at first glance. It's about doing something that might seem too far of a stretch, and then finding ways to make it a reality. It's having the foresight to see an end result in spite of all the potential hazards and obstacles trying to obscure your view, and then choosing a path to get you to the result.

The most important things I've learned about creating a vision over the years are to think bigger than you should, and not to be overwhelmed. It's easy to shatter your faith in yourself or a project when it seems too large, too intimidating. If you can convince yourself that it just might be possible, then it will become possible. From there, you have to take it in bite-sized pieces. Looking at the whole thing is often times too much to stomach. Even thinking about the next few hours can be too much. Instead, you just concentrate on the next step in front of you.

Most of my success in life has come because I've been able to hold a vision, by myself or as part of a team. I've always wanted to take on nontraditional projects, to accomplish things that there are no templates for. Too many of us lose that exploring spirit when we're young. We forget we don't have to do things the way those before us did. Pioneers can only succeed by taking on challenges that haven't been conquered or sometimes even recognized before. This means taking risks. There might be high consequences for failure, or maybe you don't even know what will happen if you fail.

Hundreds of times, I've found myself pasted against the side of a rock, in a safe, comfortable spot. I can't see the next move, and my body wants to remain where it is, rather than risk the fall. But the only way to move forward is to let go and reach above into the darkness. It's scary and it's hard, but there is always another grip out there. You can either take a chance and look for it, or be stuck inside your own fear. There's simply no way around this if you want to do something extraordinary. You can't succeed, can't climb the mountains in your life, without the occasional fall.

MountainVision

Erik and I knew the risks we were taking by setting our sites on doing something spectacular, but we also knew we had a chance to change the way people saw us, and the way we saw ourselves. We decided we weren't going to just climb a mountain; we were going to climb the biggest mountain on our side of the world. We were going to Denali ... The Great One.

With the goal of climbing Denali set firmly in our minds, Erik and I started to think of ways we could train for what would be a mammoth task. We had put this massive goal in our minds, and now it was time to break it into smaller parts. Although neither of us had been to Alaska, we knew we couldn't just show up and expect to climb the highest peak in North America. Some experienced groups never made it to the top, and plenty of them lost their lives even trying.

We set about training heavily in the Rockies. Nearly every weekend, Erik and Sam would drive to Colorado and work on mountaineering techniques with me. During the week, I would continue climbing and preparing myself mentally for the months to come, constantly guiding him in my imagination.

As fall turned to winter, the weather got harsh. We started to work on cold climate techniques, knowing that we'd have to face the same kind of ice and blizzard conditions in Alaska. As the months wore on, we decided that it was time to get out of Colorado and attempt something that wasn't in our backyard.

After scouting out some possibilities from maps and mountaineering books, we decided on Mount Rainer. It was March of 1995, our first big climb together. Tucked away in the backcountry of Washington State, 54 miles southeast of Seattle, Mount Rainier is the highest peak in the Cascade Range, and the most heavily glaciered in the contiguous US. At 14,411 feet, it would be considerably lower than Denali, but the other features would make for a good introduction to alpine training. Also, the picturesque mountain made a nice change of pace with its aesthetic beauty. It has long, spindly glaciers that reach all the way to the base. Trees and sharp features dot the sides that lead up towards its peaks. The summit itself is the most magnificent sight of all, marked by two overlapping volcanic craters, with a crystal blue lake embedded in the lower depression.

Rainier is a popular climbing destination, attracting thousands of mountaineers each summer. Winter ascents, however, are more challenging and dangerous, attempted by only a few groups each year. We planned our ascent for mid-March, late in the winter season. The harsh wind and blowing snow would make it a bad place to be. But, we wanted to avoid crowded areas, and this was definitely one way to keep out of the way. When we got to the park, no other teams were around. We were the only ones brave enough, or stupid enough, to risk the mountain's blustery, winter temper.

Summit day dawns on Mt. Rainier

The first day was all about suffering. The trail we followed would have been better suited for a Siberian Husky than a man. Only by slogging through mile after mile of thick, wet snow, icy temperatures, and frozen pine needles bristling into your face do you earn the right to attempt the more challenging sections. Step after step, my legs aching and burning, I crawled my way toward our first camp. I looked around to see Erik and Sam following suit. There was the distinct chance that we were going to freeze to death with smiles on our faces.

The second day brought more of the same. The sky spit on us relentlessly while we worked our way a bit higher. We were aware of little except the sensation of dragging our feet up a never-ending snow path.

Eventually, we reached the second camp, a small clearing that would give us the chance to take up the technical sections in the middle of the night. We hurriedly set out our tents and small stoves which we used to make some dinner and tea, the only source of warmth we had. With the sky throwing wave after wave of icy flakes at us, we settled in for some hot tea and excited conversation. Once we'd warmed ourselves as much as possible, we buttoned down for a short rest. We had only a few hours to sleep in the darkness until we'd need to attempt the final leg.

Through the night, the strong, stormy winds nipped and bit at our tent, but we barely noticed. Exhaustion and excitement produced a light, but restful sleep. The small handheld alarm that we'd packed went off at two in the morning. We sprang into action, collecting our gear and readying ourselves. We knew that outside the tent it was dark and bitterly cold, but we were so anxious we could barely stand not to jump out of the tent without getting our gear on first.

Following a quick snack and a few moments to adjust our gear and headlamps, we set out into the darkness. Despite the fierce terrain—jagged rocks interspersed with brittle ice walls—we were making great progress. After the first pitch, we climbed through an upward field of massive, sharply edged rocks seemingly piled endlessly one on another. From there, we moved into mixed climbing, sections of scrambling over SUV-sized stones interrupted by brief pitches that required rope climbing, and a few breaks of just heavy trudging through the snow A few hours in, morning broke and bathed the mountain in light. The sight of the orange rays breaking through the remaining pines and rocks above us was breathtaking. Better than that, the sun seemed to be burning through the clouds that had hung over us since the drive from Seattle.

With the weather breaking, our rapid pace carried us to the summit of Rainier only a few short hours later. We were ecstatic. It was our first big success together. We had come to test our training and readiness as a group, and had passed with flying colors. We paused for some celebratory photos, and took a moment to congratulate each other and bask in the fruits of our hard work.

Having accomplished our goal, we became eager to get back down the mountain to civilization. After days spent eating cold pasta from a can and frozen energy bars, we were eager to enjoy a hot meal and a warm bed. We made our way quickly through the difficult sections, scaling and belaying our way through the same jagged rocks and crumbling ice walls that had tortured us on the way up.

We'd already made our way through the difficult section of the descent when I was yanked off of my feet. One moment, I was walking along down the lightly descending ridge that would eventually lead us out of the park. In the next instant, my knees had been pulled up over my shoulders and I was sliding down fast. The area we had been moving through wasn't difficult, but the ridge twenty yards to our right extended down nearly five stories. It occurred to me that even if I survived the fall, that step might have been the last that my legs would ever make.

I could tell from the tension on our rope that Erik and Sam were falling as well. Sliding faster down the face and toward the drop, I couldn't see anything but white. The sensation of gliding over the slick snow face took me back to our training in Colorado.

The Diamond, Longs Peak in Rocky Mt National Park

On one particularly grueling weekend near Long's Peak in the Rockies, we'd spent several days preparing for this exact moment. I knew Denali would be filled with the hidden holes and depressions that could lie waiting just below the smooth ice surfaces. A single unlucky step on one of these natural traps could mean serious injury or worse.

    Sam had come with Erik out to the mountains in the dead of winter, where, day after day, we'd trek across snowy alpine valleys, tied together by rope. Unexpectedly, I'd throw myself to the ground and begin to glide across the ice, picking up speed. Erik, who would usually be looking for his next step, would be ripped from the ground he was standing on and follow me down the ice, our weight pulling Sam along for the ride. Once we had broken into a freefall down the glacier, our immediate task was to stop the slide as quickly as possible. For small slips, we might be able to use our crampons, or stop each other quickly using the ropes. For deeper falls, we'd attempt to drive our ice axes into the ground, hopefully self-arresting and stopping our momentum. We learned the real meaning of teamwork over those days. Slamming ourselves into the ice again and again until our entire bodies melted into a purple bruise, we learned to rely on each other, not just to stop sliding on the ice and end the pain, but ultimately to survive on the side of a mountain.

Now we were testing the trust we had built in the real world. The glacial ice flew under my back and then my side. I finally managed to roll over on my belly. My chin was facing down to the cold surface now, but I could finally reach my gear. With every ounce of strength in my body, I flung my axe into the ground and hoped for the best.

On the mountain, your axe is like an emergency parachute. You don't want to use it, but when you do, you really need it to work. We were slowing, but not fast enough. Desperately, I flung my axe again. Sam and Erik did the same. With a collective sigh of relief, we finally stopped.

I found my breath, and the strength to pull my hips from the ground. We took a moment to assess the situation and take a quick inventory. We were lucky. We'd only fallen about fifteen yards and no one was hurt. Our gear was strewn about the glacier, but everything was accounted for and nothing had broken. The incident had been just dire enough to freak us out.

From my new vantage point, it was clear what had happened. I had tripped, caught one of my crampons on the ice and sent us on the fall that nearly dropped us off the side of a cliff. What was my fault became our problem very quickly.

As I turned to apologize to my teammates, I realized an interesting thing. They were readjusting their equipment and collecting our gear. No one brought up why it had happened, or who should have done what. In the mountains, there's no time or room for blame. Time spent pointing fingers is time wasted. We had fallen as a team, now we would move on as a team.

I learned two important lessons on Rainier. First, there are no small steps, no places to relax on the side of a mountain. A single wrong move, even a tiny lapse in attention, can cost lives. Secondly, and more importantly, there's no substitute for a great team. Teamwork is the catalyst that transforms us into more than we are.

MountainVision

Without it, we are confined to what we can get done with our own ideas and natural gifts. But by adding our talents to others, our boundaries are expanded and eventually removed. People can accomplish wonderful things by working together, but there's no room for blame or separate agendas. When you're roped together on a mountain, your fate is connected to every other person on your team. It was up to each of us to do our best, not only for ourselves, but for each other. By sharing the same goal and by covering for each other, we were able to reach the top and come back down alive.

CHAPTER 5

LEARNING TO LEAD

That first trip to Alaska, in my mind, still feels like a vivid dream. It was so wonderful, so perfect, it hardly seems real. Like any mountain enthusiast, I had always dreamed of seeing the 49th state, but had experienced it only from books and stories. The cost and scope of such a trip seemed beyond reach. Erik and Sam had been intrigued by the idea of its vast beauty as well, and we were determined to find a way. After going through some of our options – the world's first bank heist led by a blind man, black market organ sales, a high-stakes roulette game—we decided we would look for sponsors. We had no idea how to approach anyone, but figured someone might be amused enough by what we were up to and throw some money our way.

Erik's dad, one of the most tenacious people I've ever met, took up the task for us. Besides his military experience, he had worked on Wall Street and knew how to make the kinds of inquiries and connections that could lead to actual funding. After a few weeks of scouting, he informed us that the American Foundation for the Blind, as well as some other organizations, would underwrite our expedition to Denali. Now, all there was left to do was climb the thing.

We flew from Denver to Anchorage in early June, still fresh off our ascent of Rainier, after doing some last minute training in the Rockies. Once we arrived there, I was blown away by the scale and beauty of the place. There were mountains that grew higher than any I'd ever seen, surrounded by forest that went deeper than your imagination.

From the urban comforts of Anchorage, a modern city poised on the edge of the wilderness, we set out on the road north, just over a hundred miles to Talkeetna. The small mountain town serves as a sort of pre-base camp for anyone who wants to go up Denali, or The Great One, as the native Athabascans call it. The weather around Denali is notoriously fickle, even in the summer, meaning flights to base camp can be held up indefinitely. Our giddy excitement melted into boredom as we spent day after day hanging around town, waiting for the clouds and winds to take a rest.

On our fourth afternoon, we found ourselves sitting again in the small bar that serves the summer's transient climbing population. Morning had brought thick, heavy clouds that draped the sky in a gray blanket as far as you could see in any direction.

The small pub was crowded with a combination of climbing dirtbags and rich peak baggers from around the world, all burning the days and hours until we could get a chance to move. We were passing the time debating the merits of the moose burger versus the local brew when someone shouted from the street. There was a hole in weather. As we dashed for the door, you could actually here all the planes fire up a mile away. It seemed like the entire village was making a mad dash for their flights.

Once we reached the airport, the scene only became more absurd. Dozens of pilots were screaming at their passengers, trying to will their clients to get in faster, stowing gear and calculating weight at a dizzying pace.

The planes themselves looked like movie props. Pure workhorses, they had begun life as small passenger aircraft that never grew into their extra horsepower. Like taxicabs with garbage truck engines, they gave a snarl that seemed to betray their small size. All had been glacier-modified with welded-on skis where the wheels would normally be. Seats were removed to make space for extra fuel and baggage, and any instruments deemed unnecessary luxuries for the bush had been removed for weight. Like zombies in some sort of undead aviation afterlife, they had lived out their glory days as shiny, state-of-the-art aircraft. Now, they had been stripped down and armored in the hope they could complete and survive this one task.

Quickly, we crammed ourselves, and our heavy packs into the back of the plane. With the oversized engine already snarling, our pilot glanced our way and asked about our weight, and the weight in our baggage. Unable to hear our answers over the roar around us, and agitated from having been woken from his nap a moment ago by the other pilots, he simply shrugged and began to inch the aircraft toward the runway. I was guessing there wouldn't be any in-flight meal service.

The winding flight through the bush gave way to magnificent peaks. Exotic, surreal features surrounded us in every direction. After another ten minutes, the narrow pass known as "One Shot," appeared from the mist. Taking its name from the margin of error that doesn't exist, this small corridor between the surrounding faces allowed only a slight clearance even for the small aircraft that flew the base camp route. The pilots were known to say a small prayer before attempting to wriggle through, as several had lost their lives over the years.

Once we'd cleared the other side, the glacier landing strip came into view. Looking more like a glacial tongue than a place to land a plane, the actual runway was a snow-packed trail sloping upward and ending abruptly with a stone wall. The pilot brought the plane to a low, slow crawl and touched down on the crunchy surface. After a few hasty minutes spent helping us unload our gear and supplies, he turned the plane and took off of the mountainside, eager to return home before being imprisoned by the clouds.

Just a hundred yards from the airstrip sat Denali base camp. The area was like a small city, with inhabitants from all around the world sharing the same goal. Alpinists from all corners of the globe were drawn to the mountain because of its prestige as the highest peak in North America. Throughout the sprawling collection of tents one could find climbers from the lower 48 states, Asia, Europe, and a few from even farther away. The rich brew of languages and anticipation filled the air in every direction.

While it brings international flavor to the base camp, the attention Denali receives is a mixed bag. The fame of being the highest point on the continent pulls in many types of climbers, some who are only marginally prepared for the challenge. While lots of the groups succeed, there is a tendency to underestimate the mountain.

At just over 20,000 feet, Denali seems less daunting or dangerous than some other prominent peaks. However, its proximity to the North Pole gives it some unique characteristics. Air pressure, decreased by the distance from the equator, makes oxygen much harder to come by. In addition, its arctic positioning makes it much more prone to storms than other mountains at similar elevations. Finally, because it's located inside the United States National Parks System, a network of rangers keeps an eye on things. While a wonderful resource for those who need it, a downside is that people assume they will be helped if they get into trouble. In my later years on the mountain, I came to see firsthand just how dangerous this assumption could be.

Once at base camp, we met our fourth teammate, Chris, who would become one of my greatest friends in life. He was working as a guide with a mountaineering company based in Alaska. He'd been up the mountain a few times before, and was excited about the idea of working with us and helping Erik reach the summit.

The idea was simple: I would guide Erik and Chris would be in charge of managing us up Denali. We had corresponded frequently by phone in the weeks before the trip, but had never met. As our plane turned and moved toward its departure, he walked over from his tent to introduce himself. With our sunglasses on, it would be impossible for him to know which of us was Erik. I was the closest to him, and decided to have some fun. Chris walked over and extended his hand in my direction. I did my best blind impression, pretending to feel my way out in front of me, and proceeded to reach out and grab him by the privates. As I shook "hands" with him, the shock on his face was priceless. He had absolutely no idea how to react, looking from one of us to the next with a confused expression. After a moment, I pulled my sunglasses down and winked.

Chris fit perfectly into our team. Besides being blessed with a wonderful sense of humor, he has a natural strength and intuitive sense of how to navigate alpine environments. After the real introductions and some preliminary talk about our route, we set about organizing ourselves for the three weeks to come.

The climb itself was magnificent. The first day or two consisted of hiking up the winding glacier that makes up Denali's lower terrain. Because we'd spent so much of the past year either alone or in our familiar locales, I had forgotten how people would react to Erik. All around base camp and the surrounding areas, where we spent our days knotted tightly next to other groups, we would receive strange looks. Either directly, or out of the corners of their eyes, the other teams would spy us leading our blind friend along the path. While their skeptical looks were understandable, I worried they would distract us from the goal of getting up and down safely. Thankfully, as we moved higher the congestion of the lower altitudes gave way to more space where we could concentrate on the tasks at hand.

Oddly enough, our early trouble on the mountain was heat. Even though Denali is nestled in a range just south of the Arctic Circle, the sun glared down on us at every step and from every angle, reflecting off the glacier that overwhelmed the landscape. The sight of so much sun coming off water, snow and ice was visually deafening. We were tiring quickly each day, often stripping down to the bare minimums of clothing, sometimes less, to endure the warmth. Ultimately, with the help of the Alaskan midnight sun, we started to climb at night. Dusk to dawn, we hiked and scrambled our way through a spectacular terrain bathed in orange, the sun lowering but never setting above us. Traveling at night proved to be safer as well. Glaciers, which move and crack under the afternoon heat, would rest while we tread over them.

MountainVision

Nearly three weeks passed as we moved up and across the mountain. We weren't the fastest team, but made better time than could have been expected. Erik handled the altitude and new terrain brilliantly. While the rest of the team soaked up the scenic views and passages that seemed to be around every turn, he absorbed the sights, sounds and smells you just couldn't find at sea level. For the first time in any of our lives, we had a sense of being on a big adventure. We were loving every second of it.

Our ascent was halted by weather at the final camp, 17,000 feet above sea level. For three days, we waited. The summit was tantalizingly close, only an eight-hour climb above us. As we waited, we had to conserve food, aware that we only had a couple days' spare provisions. Worry began to set in. If the weather didn't break in a few days, we would be forced to turn around.

Jeff, Erik, and Sam on the summit of Denali.

Finally, on the third night, a massive earthquake (a fairly common occurrence on the mountain) shook the ground beneath us and freed avalanches that roared down the mountainside below us. Quakes triggering falling slopes of snow can be disastrous, but this one turned out to be a good omen. Deep into the night, the weather broke. We were clear to ascend the summit. As fate would have it, we left early in the morning on June 27, 1995—Helen Keller's birthday.

Sam, Erik, Chris, and I set out eagerly, smiling beneath our down coats and heavy packs. That night was long, but we were all so excited it seemed effortless. I don't think any of us could believe we were really going to make it. As our triumph became more and more inevitable, the buzz in my bones became almost unbearable. To control my excitement, I focused on one step after another. I went step-by-step, almost mad with happiness. Then, as if I'd reached the end of my neighborhood block, I was standing on the summit, the highest point in North America, with a blind man at my side.

The local NBC affiliate had sent an airplane up to film us for coverage on NBC Nightly News. Standing on the peak, we could hear it flying in the distance, circling our position.

As we waved hello to what we imagined would be our new, adoring fans, Erik leaned over and asked, "Do you think they'll know which one I am?" It would be hard to tell with all of us wearing the same red suits.

"Sure." I replied. "You're the only one waving in the wrong direction."

With a chuckle, I turned my friend around toward the plane and we shared a spectacular moment, the culmination of all our hard work. It would be the first of many to come in the following years.

Mountain climbing is a perverse endeavor. It takes a different kind of person to decide they would rather drag themselves through days or weeks of pain on the side of some cold rock than stay at home in a warm bed with their loved ones. Depending on your point of view, we either have a unique idea of a good time or a massive personality defect. Either way, a side effect of the lifestyle is the development of a sick sense of humor. Part of it has to do with the climbing machismo, but part of it is a normal human response to the pain and misery we put ourselves through. Positive pessimism is a great example. It's an idea we came up with accidentally, but it has served us well over the years.

The idea began on our trip to Denali. Being stuck at high camp was a miserable time. We were parked on the only spot with any real cover, a relatively flat patch of hard rock and ice beneath a stone outcropping. We sat around for days eating cold food out of tin cans, waiting for the weather to break. Sleep was nearly impossible, with the whipping winds and tough ground doing their best to keep us awake. When we were able to catch some rest, we'd often wake up to find that the ice beneath us had melted into a small glacial pool, or that the smell of unwashed bodies in the tent had become unbearable. We'd all had it.

By the third afternoon, I wondered if we would start to crack. In order to break the tedium, we decided to press on. We'd been hoping to make some headway despite the storm, but didn't seem to be making any progress upward.

Chris was leading us up a dark, miserable glacier, when he turned and uttered, "It's cold out here, but at least it's windy" A slow smile curled up from the corner of his mouth. In spite of our shared tension, each of us chuckled for a moment.

"We've been climbing all day, but at least we're lost," Erik added. This brought a new round of laughs.

"Last night, I found a hole in my sleeping bag, but at least I got frostbite," was my contribution.

Sam had left us minutes before to relieve himself off the trail. But now, from twenty yards away, we could hear him shout, "It's twenty below, but at least I'm partially naked!"

For the next few days, whenever the team seemed to be down, someone would invent a new positive pessimism. For us, it became a way to laugh at ourselves and the downside of an unpleasant reality. Things aren't always great; they won't always be how you want them to be. The best thing to do is laugh.

I think learning not to take ourselves so seriously has been a secret of our success, and other people seem to agree. Ever since I first mentioned it in a speech years ago, the response has been overwhelming. Nearly every day I get a note from someone who is taking the idea of positive pessimism and making it work for them: "I get micromanaged, but at least my boss is an idiot." Or "The company is downsizing, but at least my assistant is still worthless." I think it's great. The next time you find yourself in a tough spot, try to find the fun in it.

And remember, life may be hard, but at least you'll die in the end.

Approaching the Moose's Tooth, Alaska Range

MountainVision

Fifteen miles southeast of Denali is another famous mountaineering destination. Like the Diamond in Colorado, the Moose's Tooth is not familiar to tourists, but many climbers are familiar with it. Also, like the Diamond, it has a name that seems wholly appropriate. A giant granite mountain jutting out from the Alaska Range, it looks like a broken tooth protruding from the glaciated terrain around it. A stone face flanked by white couloirs, deep gorges packed in with snow and ice, completes the image.

The Tooth sits like a little sister, scowling and defiant to all who climb her larger, more popular sibling. While not nearly as high, it has an intense and demanding geometry that make for a faster, but tougher climb. As the pilot had explained to me on our flight from Talkeetna to Denali base camp, it's a place "to test your manhood." I'd dismissed the shorter peak, staring me down from our aircraft window, as a curiosity. But now, a year later, I found myself aching to try it.

I rounded up a couple of my Colorado climbing buddies, Jon and Chad. After hearing all of my stories from Denali for a year, they were anxious to give Alaska a try themselves. We gathered up the money we'd need for airfare and supplies and started making preparations. Once May came around, we were on our way.

The journey through Anchorage and to the small village of Talkeenta was as breathtaking as I'd remembered. Just being back in Alaska was invigorating, and my travel partners were obviously soaking it up as well. I could see their eyes widen every time we passed into a new scenic area, as enraptured with the expansive backcountry as I was. Upon reaching our destination, we were blessed with clear weather. Not wanting to squander the opportunity, we departed as quickly as possible on our flight into the wilderness.

Our flight to Moose's Tooth was similar to the trip to Denali base camp. The same kind of glacier-modified plane rose gingerly into the air, pulling us through the sky over forests and lakes until we were in the midst of crystal peaks and snow-packed ridges. This time, however, instead of continuing toward the mountain dominating the horizon ahead, we turned north and touched down on a rugged strip of ice no more than a quarter-mile long.

A far cry from the cosmopolitan feel of Denali base camp, we were utterly alone on the Ruth Glacier. I couldn't be sure, but I was pretty convinced we'd reached the actual geographic middle of nowhere. Once we'd unloaded our few small bags of gear and the plane made its hasty exit, there was absolutely no one but the three of us. We had four days to get up and down. After that, the pilot would come back and pick us up, if he could.

Between the glacier where we landed and the site of our first camp was a huge crevasse field. Beneath the seemingly flat, snow-packed surface were huge holes in the earth, hiding like landmines. We roped together tightly and navigated from one area to the next, our eyes and ears straining to detect any hint of a crack in the ice.

Three nerve-wracking hours later, we reached our campsite and set up our tent. Sleep was hard to come by. Like skydivers who had just reached the ground, we were too wired to relax. The three of us, isolated and alone in the treacherous wilderness, spent most of the night in a giddy daze. We considered continuing our ascent through the night, but the sounds of avalanches tumbling above and around us dismissed the notion.

Finally, morning came and we were free to head up the mountain. We roped up and started into the long slopes of snow and toward the vertical pitches. With our crampons biting into the hard snow before us, we gently traversed our course, gradually working our way upward. The packed snow below us seemed to be in better shape than could be expected, but I was still wary. As the most experienced climber in the group, I felt I should point out and avoid potential hazards, even if it seemed trivial. After a couple of hours, Jon and Chad seemed to be tiring of my cautious mother routine, rolling their eyes slightly as I'd advise moving more slowly here or taking extra precaution there.

And so, as we approached a benign-looking patch of thickly packed, frozen-over snow, I asked Jon to plant a picket. The long spike, with a hole for our rope to pass through, would help to arrest us in the event of a fall. Jon shrugged impatiently and planted it into the ground. With our precaution in place, the team began to move forward. I led the way, followed by Jon, with Chad in the rear.

I was through the small patch and examining the route ahead when I heard the faint crack. Before I could turn and tell Jon to stay still, snow had rushed beneath my knees and was carrying me down the ridge. The rope tugged and released as our picket was ripped from the ground, unable to support the full weight of three climbers.

My mind raced to assess the danger of the fall we were in. The slope wasn't extreme; there was no risk of falling off of any cliff or ridge. Still, the sheer volume of powder falling into us and picking up speed had me concerned. It was lighter as it sped down the hill, but once we stopped, the molecules would condense. What was now light and fluffy would become heavy and thick, like concrete. If it covered our heads, we'd surely suffocate. Worse yet, if it buried us to our elbows we'd be unable to dig out—we'd freeze to death, and be awake the whole time. I wasn't sure if my companions were aware of this, but as I heard them struggle to stay above, I figured they had an idea of the danger.

I rolled over and attempted to swim through the tide, working furiously to keep my arms above. Unable to stay horizontal, I ended up nearly standing. Like a furious whitewater rapid, the rush of snow could knock me over, drowning me in it. Just as quickly as the realization came to me, however, the slide stopped. The tiny avalanche that had been triggered by the snow bridge's collapse was over. It had carried us forty or fifty yards, but we were none worse for the wear. I was only buried to my waist, and I could see that Jon and Chad were even better off than I was.

Using my hands as scoops, I cleared the snow from around me. I reached Jon, who was shaking the last bits of powder from his coat, first. We exchanged a pair of did you see that looks, and then had a laugh. We'd fallen prey to one of the mountain's unforeseen dangers and lived.

Chad, however, didn't seem to share our good spirits. The look on his face was one of shock. He'd come to Alaska for an adventure, but didn't want to pay with his life. Until that moment, he hadn't realized how high the stakes really were. I knew everyone handled these things mentally in their own way, so I gave him some space while I collected the loose bits of gear and food that had fallen off of me and were scattered around the drift. Jon did the same.

Finally, after a few moments, the three of us gathered. I pointed up to a spot on the ridge near where our slide had begun and explained that we could probably get back in an hour. Jon nodded, but Chad said nothing. I took my first steps back toward our route, reminding them that we'd been lucky and would have to continue to be careful. It was nearly a minute before Jon and I realized that Chad hadn't followed us. We made our way back over to him, fearing he might have an injury we hadn't discovered initially. When we reached him, we saw that his problem wasn't physical.

He looked at us both, one and then the other. "You guys still want to go up?"

Jon and I exchanged glances. Was he serious? We'd spent a huge amount of money on flights and preparations. We'd come thousands of miles to do this. The slide had been an unlucky break, but everyone was fine. If anything, the route was actually safer now that we'd already sprung the trap that had been waiting for us. Besides, the plane wasn't coming back for us for at least three more days. What else were we going to do?

"Well... sure." I said as delicately as I could. Then I laid out all the reasons to continue.

"I understand." Chad said. "But I don't have a good feeling about this. That picket shouldn't have pulled." He looked toward Jon now.

I could see Jon getting red in the face. He'd planted the picket, and he'd been the one to fall. Still, he could never have known that under his feet was a thin layer of snow covering an air bubble. I'd walked over the same spot only moments before. It was nobody's fault, and we all knew it.

I stepped in before angry words came out. "Pickets aren't supposed to hold three people. Sometimes they can help and sometimes they can't. There was nothing under that ice to bore into." This seemed to quell Jon's anger, but not Chad's fear.

We persuaded Chad to go through to the next camp, which we could set up after a short hike. Once we made camp, we sat down to talk about our progress and decide what to do. I was afraid that Chad, overcome by what had happened, would decide not to go further and miss out on his chance to take part in an adventure we'd been planning for months. But after more than an hour of discussion, it became apparent that he had no interest in continuing on. With no way to get back to civilization, he offered to stay in camp while Jon and I went on.

As reluctant as we were to leave him, it was too tempting an offer to resist. Chad would be safe in camp, and we didn't know when we'd ever get a chance to return. Two people would be able to move much more quickly than three, especially without the spare gear and provisions we could now leave at camp. After Chad's assurances that he'd be fine, we decided not to wait for dawn. We set out across the rock face into the channel of snow under the midnight sun.

Moving through pitch after pitch, surrounded by the idyllic oranges and blues of the glacial ice leading to the top, we climbed in harmony with the mountain and each other. The closer we got to the top, the steeper the face became. Finally, we came to the final challenge—a massive, sixty-degree couloir extending thousands of feet to the summit. The snow was packed enough to step and dig into, but not hard enough to hold ice screws, even at night. If we wanted to finish, we'd have to free climb. There would be no tools or safety gear to save us, we were at the mercy of our hands and our feet.

Without a word, I began to make the first step. After twelve hours of scratching and clawing our way upward, Jon and I had reached an understanding. We were going to the top. Nothing was going to stop us.

After a few moves up, Jon broke the silence. "Be careful," he said.

I looked back down to him. Of course, be careful. Why would he have said that? All at once, I got his meaning. We weren't using ice screws to catch us should we fall, but we were still roped in together. If I fell, there was as much chance that I'd take him down too as there was that he'd be able to stop my fall. I nodded to him and continued up.

For hours, we went on. We took turns leading the sections, entrusting our lives to each other. Morning broke and we continued to strain up. I was aware of being both exhausted and exhilarated, but the only thought that filled me was reaching the top.

When we reached the summit, no words were spoken. Jon and I both knew what we had been through together, what we'd both risked to make it to that moment.

When we finally made our way back down to camp eighteen hours later, I expected Chad to be sour. I thought he would have regretted his decision not to go all the way. Instead, he congratulated us and asked about our ascent. He was impressed with the story, but didn't seem to be bothered by not having been a part of it.

For anything in life, there are different levels of commitment. It's up to each of us to decide what we're willing to put into something. For Jon and me, the goal was reaching the top, despite the risks. In Chad's case, he realized he enjoyed climbing as a hobby, but it wasn't worth the heavy risks to pursue it as far as we had. That's all right. It's better to discover your level of dedication to something and trust in that than it is to blindly follow those around you. Whatever you do in life, find your commitment to it and follow that to the top ... or not.

My time in Alaska had given me a love of the place, and I was dying to return. Luckily, I'd remained friends with one of the rangers we'd met during our ascent of Denali. The next year, he invited me back to work on the mountain with the National Parks Service. I spent two summers working around the park — repairing trails, digging latrines, and rescuing climbers in need—having a fantastic time and saving money for school.

The following year, during the summer of 1998, I went back to Denali to work as a guide. My years as a ranger had made me familiar with the mountain, and I wanted to stay outdoors as much as possible before I left for The Medical College of Pennsylvania. I'd decided to return to school to become a Physician Assistant. While I was excited about fulfilling my dream of working in medicine, I knew the long hours in classrooms would be a far cry from the alpine lifestyle I'd come to love.

Chris was still taking clients up Denali at that the time, and got me on as a guide with his company. During one grueling stretch, we were scheduled to lead two trips back to back. It would be exhausting work to climb the mountain, return to base camp, and then scale it again. Especially when you considered that we didn't just have ourselves to take care of, but also our clients. The energy we'd spend on carrying extra gear on our backs, not to mention cooking, giving instruction and keeping everyone as safe as possible, would ensure that it wouldn't be an easy six weeks. Despite the challenge, we were eager to get back on the mountain and meet up with our clients.

We arrived at base camp a couple of days before our group to begin preparations for the long trip. As we spent the first day getting settled, word got around that a Park Service ranger had fallen from a high altitude. No one could find him, but a few climbers had definitely seen him slip over the edge of a ravine. The ledge where he'd been standing went down several thousand feet, and there wasn't a lot of hope that he'd survived. With my years on the mountain, I knew how easy it would be for someone to make a simple mistake that could cost them their life. I hoped that he'd be alright, or at least not in pain.

On our third day at base camp, the first group of climbers had arrived on the glacier and were taking in the pristine beauty of the Alaska range. The sun burned brightly as morning turned into a clear, crisp May afternoon. Most of the clients on the expedition were foreigners, and they were clearly excited to be on the other side of the world tackling North America's highest peak. As we took an inventory of persons and equipment, they chattered and giggled and laughed amongst themselves. Once we were satisfied that everyone and everything was present, we took a brisk pace through the path of packed snow that would lead to the first night's camp. Now that we were underway, their excitement was palpable. Then, something happened that would ruin our good spirits.

Late in the afternoon I'd heard radio chatter that a group thought they'd spotted the fallen ranger, but couldn't reach him by foot. It was eventually decided that the park service would send out "The Denali Lama," the Park Service helicopter with a specially attached grabber to try to retrieve him. The grabber was a valuable tool, enabling pilots to pick up equipment, debris, and even people with the use of a hydraulic arm that would deploy below the helicopter. It looked a bit like the arcade game where people use a mechanical arm to win stuffed animals, although this claw was much larger and more menacing.

From the air, the crew was able to confirm that the ranger had indeed fallen over the side of the crevasse. He was killed instantly by the impact, but had been lying frozen and face down for days. Now, the helicopter would recover him and bring him back for burial.

Flying a helicopter through the Alaska range, even without the grabber attached, is a dangerous and demanding job. Narrow corridors, unpredictable winds, and poor visibility can lead to accidents in a heartbeat. The talented men and women who fly these missions manage some of the risk by going low and slow through familiar routes. As luck would have it, we'd stopped our group of clients in a small flat area that lay directly under the chopper's path that day.

MountainVision

Our party, exhilarated by the fantastic weather and scenery, had stopped to take a rest and some photos. When we heard the sound of the aircraft approaching, the clients began to point with big smiles. They wanted to see the chopper close up. It rounded a corner and slowly floated into view. However, their eyes were not drawn to the shiny aircraft, but to the dead ranger staring back at them from a hundred feet up. He glided through the air, arms and legs still frozen in his bloody down outfit. For climbers, the mountain rangers are like superheroes. They're the ones who tame the hills and keep everyone in line. But as tough as this ranger had been, the mountain had chewed him up and spit him back out.

Jeff and other Rangers performing a rescue on the Denali Lama

One by one, the smiles turned into expressions of horror as they took in the reality of what had happened. And then, just as quickly, they each began to internalize his fate. After all, if this professional ranger who worked and lived his days on this mountain had fallen to his death, how safe were they? The unspoken question weighed heavily on all of them.

There was nothing to say, except to explain that on the mountain things could happen and, because of this, we needed to be very careful. I told them I'd been around Denali for years, as had Chris, without incident. I could see, however, that my words wouldn't take away their concerns.

No one who comes to scale North America's highest peak is new to mountaineering. All of our clients had done some climbing, and many of them had managed peaks much more technically challenging and dangerous. We still had the same experienced group we'd had moments ago. We still had the same great equipment and the same perfect weather. The only thing that we'd lost was our group's confidence, but we wouldn't be able to go all the way without it.

In the weeks after that moment, the whole complexion of the party changed irreversibly. The laughs died down. Everyone got a little quieter. Smiles turned to pained expressions of fear. Nothing Chris or I said seemed to make a difference. The farther we went along, the more down our clients seemed.

As we neared the high camp in preparation for a summit attempt, the weather grew severe, as it had my first time on Denali. We waited days through the bitter cold for the sky to open up and permit us to reach the top. The wind and snow beat down on our tents day and night. Finally, the group came to our tent and announced that they would like to head down. They no longer cared about making it to the summit, they just wanted to return home. They had come from around the world for this opportunity, but now all they wanted was to get off the mountain and catch a flight back to Talkeetna.

On the surface, there are many reasons why a team might not succeed. Illness, bad weather, a shortage of supplies, or even simple fatigue can sideline a climbing expedition. Certainly, after days of waiting for the snow and wind to clear up, we had those issues. Still, they aren't what kept us from the top. The truth is, we had picked up another team member that very first day. With every step of every section, the dead ranger was going with us. Mentally we pulled him along each day until the weight was too great for us to bear.

The next week, we led our second group up the mountain. They were the same kinds of climbers, facing the same kinds of weather and challenges. But, three weeks later we reached the top. I truly believe that the only thing separating those groups was that one had their confidence shattered by an outside event.

MountainVision

You can inherit someone else's fear, or their failure. Any time you try to do something exceptional in this world, you're bound to come across or be reminded of those who didn't make it. It's easy to accept their fate as your own, especially if they seem to be stronger or more talented than you are. But no matter what their reasons for not making it, they aren't your reasons. You have to learn to recognize the mistakes and misfortunes of others without making them your own, it's the only way any of us can keep making progress. Heroes fall sometimes. That doesn't mean you have to.

Towards the tail end of a Denali summer, Chris and I found ourselves guiding a dozen clients up the mountain in search of the elusive summit. Our group had fought through two weeks of sloppy terrain and the late summer blizzards that typically pound the mountain. We had just set up camp at fourteen-thousand feet, where we and our clients would spend a couple of days for much-needed rest and acclimatization. After fourteen days of hard charging, going uphill eight or ten hours a day with seventy pounds strapped to my back, I was relieved to be resting. I could tell from the way Chris was moving as we settled our clients in and prepared our own tent that the long climbing season was catching up with him as well.

Once we had melted some snow for fresh water and prepared dinner for everyone we finally crawled into our bags for some sleep. After about an hour of the kind of clear, sound sleep that only utter exhaustion can produce, I woke up to hear a clamor around camp. I wondered which of our clients would be up and making so much noise in the night.

As my attention slowly came back to the waking world, I could make out Roger Robinson's voice. Roger was head of all the rangers in Denali National Park, the man responsible for keeping the park and its staff functioning smoothly. I'd come to know him well over the years. If he was excited about something, it was important. I crawled out of my bag hoping to help Roger find what he needed and fade back into slumber as quickly as possible. But before I could get my boots on and step outside, he was zipping open the entrance to our tent.

Roger had heard Chris and I were on the hill and had come to ask a favor. "I'm sorry to bother you guys," he blurted out, "but we're short on people and we need some help."

I stirred Chris awake as Roger explained the situation. A pair of climbers had reported a fall down a route called the Orient Express. Denali had several sections that were notorious for falls. The rangers had given each of them colorful names based on the origins of climbers who frequently fell down them. In addition to the Orient Express, the Autobahn and the Champs Elysees were frequent trouble spots.

This accident seemed to have happened like most on the mountain do. The team had reached the summit and failed to maintain their focus on the descent. As a result, at least one of the team members had slipped and gone over a ledge into a half-mile freefall. The park rangers were shorthanded, and they needed help retrieving and treating the injured.

As tired as we were, we knew we had to go.

Mountaineers work by a code that basically amounts to the Golden Rule: you help out those who need it, no matter what. It's a dangerous sport, and we try to look out for each other for two reasons. First, it's the right thing to do; but second—and just as important—is that you never know when you may be the one in need of help. So without delay, Chris and I dressed and gathered a minimal amount of gear to bring on the four-hour trek to the area where the climbers had landed.

I felt anxious about explaining our departure to our clients. They had spent large amounts of money securing our services, and now we needed to leave them for the night. But to my relief, they immediately understood and said they would fend for themselves until morning.

MountainVision

It was approaching midnight as Chris and I climbed up the icy slopes several hundred vertical yards between our camp and the fall zone. The midnight sun hung low on the horizon, throwing a blue glow off the surface for miles in any direction. When we arrived at the depression where the fallen climber had settled, we saw that a "hasty team," a group of mountain EMTs carrying light medical equipment, had just arrived.

There were two injured climbers. Both were breathing, but one had massive internal injuries and would need to be evacuated right way. The other, despite having some assorted injuries, including a shattered ankle, at least seemed to be in stable condition.

It is difficult enough to make your way up or across a mountain like Denali. It's much tougher to carry someone else along with you. The series of pitches that had taken us four hours to manage on the first leg had to be traversed at a painfully slow pace on our return. Some sections had to be avoided altogether, as we wouldn't be able to move through with an immobilized patient. Others simply required small steps and minute movements to find a way without jostling the injured man or harming ourselves in the process.

Like snails moving through sand, we inched our way along until at last we were able to deposit the patient at the high camp medical tent. By the time we'd made the short walk back to our own tent, more than eighteen hours had past. Our clients had taken care of themselves well enough, but we had missed our rest day. There was nothing to do except catch a few hours of sleep before we broke camp in the morning. But once again our rest was short-lived.

Just as I was settling into my bag, before I even had time to close my eyes, I heard Roger's voice again. I ignored it for a moment, thinking I must have been hearing things out of exhaustion. But when I heard him call a second time, I realized he had returned to our camp. I stuck my head out of my tent to see him approaching.

"Guys, I am so sorry. Look, I know how wiped out you are, but there's been another fall. Sounds as if a few Brits have fallen down the same section of the Orient Express."

Jeff Evans

    Without a word, Chris and I made ready to leave once more. A few of our clients had overheard and offered that no explanation was needed. They would simply wait until we could return. As the sun made its way nearer to the horizon, we set out again through the blue fields and walls of ice in front of us toward the injured party.

    Amazingly, the injured pair had landed in nearly the same spot as we'd been at the night before. The two victims were members of the British Army who had come to the mountain as part of a military climbing exercise. In a perverse showing of the buddy system, one had fallen and taken his roped-in partner with him. Together, they'd slid down the steep face and landed close to where our previous patients had been. I couldn't believe it. The odds of two pairs of climbers slipping at precisely the same point, falling thousands of feet while careening off of rocks, ice, and other features, and then landing in the same depression had to be astronomical.

    We caught up to the hasty team en route and could see the bodies lying motionless less than twenty-five feet from the first fall. Despite their good fortune of falling onto a bed of powder, neither seemed to be moving. Moreover, the streaks of blood marking their path downward weren't encouraging.

    Cold and exhausted, the four of us stopped to take a better look through high-powered binoculars. We peered through the lenses for five minutes and neither fallen climber so much as moved. I sighed. It was unfortunate that we wouldn't be able to save them, but accidents on the mountain weren't uncommon. During the busy summer months, there could be as many as three falls a week. If these guys hadn't made it, we'd send a helicopter when the weather was clear.

    We were about to leave the hasty team to go forward and confirm the victims' fate when one of the medics yelled out. An unusual mix of shock and amusement came over his face. "You'll never believe this," he exclaimed as he handed me his binoculars.

    If I hadn't seen it with my own eyes, I wouldn't have. The smaller climber had stood up and was shaking his head. He looked severely disoriented, but he was actually standing on his own two feet.

We yelled at the top of our lungs for him to stop, but he either couldn't hear us or didn't register our words. He began taking one shaky step after another, bumbling his way forward. What had begun as amazing was about to end tragically. He was in a daze, walking straight toward a ledge five yards in front of him. We kept screaming as he continued shuddering forward. Suddenly he stopped, as if realizing what he was about to do, and teetered backward. We all let out a sigh of relief. Then, without warning or hesitation, he took a step forward and disappeared into a crack below. We couldn't see where he'd fallen, but it didn't seem important. He'd been lucky once, but ultimately, not lucky enough.

Still, we wondered about his companion. After all, if the shorter climber had survived, perhaps his partner had as well. We gathered up our gear and began to climb our way toward his body. About two minutes later, with roughly half a mile separating us from the spot where they'd landed, Chris stopped mid-step and uttered a profanity.

I followed his gaze until I realized what he saw and threw out a four-letter tribute of my own. The shorter climber was up again. He'd survived a nearly 3,000-foot fall, gotten up to walk, fallen off a 45-foot ice cliff, and now was making his way toward us. We screamed frantically at him to stay still, but our words didn't seem to find him. He simply stumbled forward with a blank expression on his face.

Now just a couple hundred yards in the distance, we allowed ourselves to consider the possibility that he might make it to us. We set about navigating our way through the fragile ice field with its cracks, holes and false surfaces, all the while shouting at the top of our lungs. With every ounce of volume and strength we could find, we begged him to stay put. We were no more than 60 feet away when he vanished. It was as if a trap door had opened beneath his feet. He had stepped on a snow bridge and it gave way, trapping him in a cold pit that might extend down ten feet, or hundreds of yards.

Jeff Evans

We scrambled over to the depression and looked inside. I saw something that will stay with me until the day I die. The small man, battered and disoriented, was using his frozen hands like ice axes. He chipped away at the snow and ice around him, clawing his way up to the top of the ridge. He seemed to have lost all conscious thought and was driving forward on pure instinct. After some quick rope work, Chris and I were able to pull him up and sit him down on the ground. Then, as we had the night before, we bandaged and packaged the patient as best we could and made our way back to the medical tent at camp.

More by luck than skill, our patient survived the ordeal. We found out later that he had just been married in England, and the thought of losing his new wife was too much for him. Even now, I'm taken aback when I think of the grit and determination he showed. That man was going to walk back to base camp no matter how many cliffs were in his way. Just as shocking, his partner escaped the fall with nothing more than a shattered ankle and a blow to the head that had rendered him unconscious.

As gratifying as it was to have helped save a life, I was worried for and about our clients. We'd been gone from camp nearly three days and were in no shape to continue climbing right away. The men and women in our group had paid a lot of money to try to reach the top of the mountain, and Chris and I had been keeping them from it. The small British climber had reminded me about the power of the human will, however my clients reminded me of the depth of human spirit.

As we dragged ourselves into the collection of tents where they'd been holed up for days, they greeted us enthusiastically. Rather than scold us, they insisted on making us dinner and tea. We were being paid to take care of them on the mountain, but now they had decided to take care of us.

For the next 24 hours, our group waited patiently while Chris and I recouped from over 48 straight hours of hard climbing with no sleep. On the second day, with our bodies and minds restored, we led our clients up to high camp, and then the summit later that week.

MountainVision

I will always have a special place in my heart for that group of clients. For all of the money spent on the trip of a lifetime, they were happy to delay their adventure for other people they didn't even know. They understood what true adventure, and true humanity, are all about.

So many of us spend our lives in a self-absorbed bubble. We get too wrapped up in our own issues to even acknowledge the struggles around us, much less help. Mountaineers have always gone by a code: if you see someone in trouble, you help. It doesn't matter if you're 100 feet from the summit and you've spent 70,000 dollars to get there. It's the right thing to do.

It saddens me to know how many climbers seem to have forgotten this rule. The news has been rife in recent years with stories of incapacitated people passed over and left to die near the summits of Everest and the other big mountains, while others, sometimes their own companions, go on to make the summit. Instead of teams helping each other get to the top and back, there are loose confederations of people all pursuing their own goals. This is a losing approach to teamwork, and a terrible way to go about life.

There is a great feeling that comes along with reaching the summit, but a deeper joy that comes from being able to help someone else out. You don't have to climb a mountain to find a person in your life who could use a hand. The Golden Rule isn't just for mountain climbers, and you don't have to save someone's life to make a difference. Even a small sacrifice can have a huge effect on another person, and you might be surprised at the joy you find within a good deed done. When the chance comes, try to be a real hero. Stay focused on your goals, but don't let them come at the expense of those who need you.

Erik and I took a brief break from hardcore climbing following our summit of Denali. We needed some time to rest and build our strength back up. I had lost nearly twenty pounds during our time in Alaska and Erik had shed nearly as many himself. Besides, after a year of heavy training, we both had other responsibilities to attend to. I was off to school, and Erik had become something of a national hero. The piece on NBC Nightly News had triggered an avalanche of coverage from television, magazines, and the Internet. Everyone wanted to talk to us, from indie film directors, to People magazine.

While we were grateful for the attention, by the next year we were eager to move on and try something different. Encouraged by our Denali success, Erik and I started searching for a new challenge. We decided to make a run at El Capitan, a granite monolith standing in California's Yosemite Valley. We had taken down North America's highest mountain, now we wanted to climb the tallest rock face. The timing seemed perfect. It was the summer of 1996, and I had just finished my first summer patrol in Alaska. Rather than go straight back to school, I used a bit of my savings to fly to San Francisco. Sam and Erik met me at the airport, and we set out for several weeks of hard training.

"El Cap" would be different from anything we'd scaled before. Unlike a lot of mountains, there simply aren't any easy ways up. Nor are there any sections where you can relax. It only rises about 3,500 feet off the ground, but you have to fight for every single inch. More than any other American climbing landmark, the stubborn stone face has a long history of denying those who attempt it. Indeed, for several decades after the first attempts at the summit, a climb to the summit was considered impossible.

It would be a change of pace from the last two years in almost every conceivable way.

MountainVision

If Denali had been a marathon in the snow, then El Cap would be a sprint through an obstacle course. We had been used to training for a big, alpine peak washed in snow and ice.

El Capitan, Yosemite National Park, California

The only way to successfully summit was to bring big heavy packs and wear the mountain down until it let you crawl to the top. By comparison, El Cap would be a deeply technical climb in scorching temperatures—a rock maze of overhanging faces, fingertip holds, and smooth walls that offered no grip. There were ghostly slabs that went up several stories without so much as a crack, much less a ledge where you could eat or sleep.

With an eye toward nearly nonstop training, the three of us rented a house in Western Yosemite. We devoted the next few weeks to honing our technical skills and adapting the methods that worked for us in Alaska to a different kind of task. Just as we'd known that Denali would test our endurance and ability to withstand the elements, El Cap would be a gauge of our raw aptitude and instinct.

We got off to a slow start. Our first target was a big stone block, protruding about 1,400 feet from the earth on the outskirts of the park. With its winding corridors rumbling right to left on the way to the top, it looked to be a nice orientation to a technical challenge.

Jeff Evans

We started up just after 7:00 a.m., alternating leads while lifting ourselves through the short pitches. The climbing was slow as each of us took our turns at the front, grinding up the sheer face that pinched our fingers and scraped our legs. By noon, we were just short of halfway up. It felt like the sun was beating down on us directly, as if it had chosen us alone to receive its torment. The heavy heat only served to slow our progress. I found myself tiring quickly and clawing at the rock with sweaty hands. The day wore on and we continued toward the top. A climb that should have taken us a few hours saw us reach the summit near sun down.

We knew we had to descend, but fatigue took hold as we took in the last of our water at the top. Finally, the sun disappeared and we began to make our way back to ground. It was Sam's turn to lead, but in the darkness he couldn't find our rappel anchors, the metal hooks that we would slide our ropes through to lower down the rock. Sam and I searched for them with our headlamps while Erik took to ground, reaching out to find them with his hands. After a few minutes, the situation started to look bleak.

It was the evening of our first day, and we were lost. As hot as the day had been, the evening alpine cold would be dangerous if we had to sleep out all night.

After some more searching, I nearly tripped over one of the anchors and we belayed our way down the side. Our spirits weren't great, but we'd been through enough together to know that every day wasn't perfect. So, without any words we headed for sleep.

We took an extra rest day after our previous debacle, and then decided to give it another try. We chose another rock that offered a similar challenge, and set out to climb. After a few minutes of preparations, we realized we were short some of the gear we'd need. The three of us debated for a few moments about who had been responsible for bringing it, until we finally agreed just to head back to the house and start over. Not wanting to lose a whole day, we sped back, gathered the missing gear, and returned as quickly as we could.

Hanging off El Cap.

Only a couple of hours had passed, but by the time we started climbing, the heat in the park was overwhelming. The stone was scorching to the touch. Even worse, the pale granite was acting as a furnace, radiating light and heat back at us.

My thoughts became slow and sluggish. I found myself daydreaming about climbing the side of a baked potato. The thought made me laugh slowly out loud. Sam, confused by my outburst, peered up at me from below. There was something odd about his face, but I couldn't put my finger on it. He was bright red, but completely dry. I felt my shirt; I was dry too. We had all stopped sweating. We were suffering from heat exhaustion.

I quickly recalled my medical training and realized our peril. In this situation, heat exhaustion could be deadly. Facing the extreme temperatures and dehydration, any of us could have a heat stroke. We were miles from the nearest road, and at least an hour from a hospital. I hollered up to Erik, who was a short ladder-length above me, that we should take some water and turn around immediately.

He turned his head toward me, but before he could reply he vomited. That was answer enough. As the contents of his stomach rained down, I started to wonder how long until we could get back home.

I ran my hands hastily over the vomit-soaked rocks, trying to find my way down as quickly as possible. Luckily, our slow progress meant that we had only a few short pitches to retreat through until we were back to our car. Once off the ropes, we huddled in the shade, making sure to finish off the contents of our water bottles. We shuttled home for some rest, but no one spoke. Our first week had seen us climb twice, and both had nearly ended very badly.

Once again, we were forced to set aside a few days for unplanned recuperation. By the beginning of the second week we were feeling stronger and ready to hit the rocks again. We decided to make a long day of several shorter formations, going up and down while concentrating on basic technique. Our movements were clumsy, but without any serious mistakes. By the afternoon, we'd all lightened up a bit. With each successful route, some of the tension of our earlier failures melted away.

For the last climb of the day, we picked a tall stone structure with twists and curves that made it look as much like modern art as a natural feature. I led the first pitch, finding my movements more easily now. Erik followed, his strong climbing instincts returning as well. Finally, Sam joined us at the top.

Once we reached the summit, we paused for a quick high five and decided to call it a day. Mirroring our ascent, I was the first to go down, followed by Erik, and then Sam. Once I'd reached the bottom, I started to take off some of my gear and give a few verbal directions to Erik. Soon, he had reached safety as well. Erik began belaying Sam down, who was removing our gear from the face as he rappelled to ground. With the day's mission firmly accomplished, I laid back into a small patch of grass, grateful for the rest.

While I was napping in the grass, Erik had been doling out small rations of rope to Sam, who would remove a piece of gear and then come down another ten feet and remove another. As the anchorman holding the line, Erik was the only thing keeping Sam from falling backward. As he rappelled down lower however, the small pile of excess rope was drying up. Unable to see the dwindling length on the ground, Erik fed Sam the last bit, which flew up toward the sky. Sensing a break in the rope's tension, Sam instinctively grabbed onto the gear he was removing, a split second before it was too late. Had it not held, he would have fallen backward to his death.

My eyes opened wide when I heard the rope slip. I looked over to Erik, who was feeling for the safety line that had flung far above him, useless without the weight to anchor it. Sam looked an ashen white, hanging backward from 60 feet above. I was able to free climb quickly to his location with a new rope in hand, but it was too late — the damage to our psyche had been done. Our first two training mishaps had been dangerous, but this one came within an inch of killing one of us.

Shaken, we returned to our rented home. No one knew what to say or think. When morning came, instead of going climbing, the three of us headed to a local coffee shop. No one had fallen the day before, but they might as well have. Our confidence in ourselves and in each other had been shattered.

We had a long, heartfelt talk that lasted for hours. As my two teammates and I aired our thoughts and fears, we realized that we had some serious questions to address. Had we been lucky on Denali? Were we good enough to keep going? Did we trust each other enough? Were we doing enough to stay safe?

One by one we weighed in. At several times in the discussion, we almost agreed to call our trip to El Cap, and maybe any future trips, off for good. The worries and concerns that came up were all serious and legitimate. Sam wasn't sure he could still trust Erik to keep him safe. Erik wasn't sure he could still trust me to be his fail safe. I didn't know if Sam was strong enough to keep going.

In the end, we decided that we could beat El Cap, but we'd have to start taking it more seriously. This wouldn't be like anything we'd done before, and we couldn't assume just because things had worked out for us last time, that they would this time. We needed to keep a better eye on each other. There was no rest; there were no times to relax as long as any of us was in danger. Our team nearly fell that day. We narrowly escaped giving into fear and mistrust. When we walked into that coffee shop, I thought we might never climb together again. Instead, by being open to each other and recommitting to our goals, we came out stronger than we'd ever been.

Five weeks later, we went to climb El Capitan. The ascent itself was somewhat unremarkable, because we'd done the hard work needed to reach the top before we showed up. It took some trial and error, but we found out we could do something that, in the beginning, had seemed beyond us.

El Cap isn't one of the world's highest summits. It's not that high off the ground, compared to a mountain like Rainer or Denali. Outside of the climbing community, the public and the press aren't familiar with it. So when we reached the summit this time, there were no cameras or microphones. But we knew what we'd put in to reach that point. We'd done it just for ourselves and, as we celebrated our small, private victory, I'd never been so proud of myself and my teammates.

The big victories aren't always the ones that people think they should be. But deep inside, you know when you've done something significant—when you've pushed yourself beyond your comfort and into a new area. Seek out those challenges, and don't be afraid of setbacks along the way. Sometimes you have to lose before you can win. A step back can be a step forward, but only if you keep at it.

When I first started working in medicine, I had a mentor. Mark was, and still is, a terrific doctor who had consistently excelled at everything he'd ever done in life. As an emergency room doctor with an undergraduate degree in engineering from MIT, he was the type of person that most parents want their kids to grow up to be. Whenever I had a problem in the hospital, or in my life, he would be the person I would see. With his sharp mind and patient demeanor, he really seemed to be capable of fixing anything. A misplaced IV here, a weird test result there, he covered it all. As a beginning Physician Assistant, there was no one better for me to count on.

Mark had moved to Colorado in his early twenties to satisfy not only his professional aspirations, but also his taste for adventure, which included some casual mountaineering. His natural enthusiasm made him a solid weekend climber. So, from time to time, we would go out together for a long day on the rocks or to hike up a fourteener. He hadn't scaled the kinds of big mountains that I had, but he loved the outdoors and kept himself in superb shape. Despite being well into his forties, I found that he rarely had trouble keeping up with me.

Around this time, I got the idea to try a route on Long's Peak that had been near the top of my list for a while. This piece of mountain was one of the most sought after alpine routes in North America because it had a bit of everything: rock, ice, technical climbing and even some scrambling. I sent an e-mail out to several of my climbing buddies, hoping to get a party together to take a long day trip. I decided to include Mark, even though I felt it was probably a bit above his technical skill level. I was sure he'd be too busy anyway, and I wanted him to feel like he was part of my inner circle of friends, which he was. I also wanted him to think I considered him to be up to the grueling challenge, which I thought he probably wasn't.

Of course, I should have known to expect the unexpected. Not only was Mark willing to go, he was the only one. And he was fired up. When he stopped me in the hospital to remind me how excited he was, I was forced to confess that I thought the route might be a bit much for him. His only rope experience to date had been various short climbs with me in Boulder. He'd gotten to the top of several local mountains, but few offered even the slightest technical challenge. This attempt on Long's would be much more intense and trying. My reluctance seemed to leave him understandably confused. After all, I'd invited him. Now that he'd accepted, I was telling him that it probably wasn't a good idea. What kind of sense did that make?

After showing the kind of steely persistence that had carried him through a top medical school, otherwise known as incessant pestering, I decided to let him come along. I reasoned that his enthusiasm would be enough to carry him through the tougher pitches and that his attitude would more than make up for any weakness as a climber.

It was hours before daybreak when we met to set up the side of the hill. At three in the morning, a climber can easily feel one of two things: the exhilaration of starting off on a new adventure, or the sheer agitation of being awake when your body screams to be in bed. I wasn't feeling exhilarated. My edginess was coming through and Mark wasn't helping.

As we initially set out in the darkness, I realized his gear wasn't up to the task. Per my instructions, he had brought crampons for the climb. The small metal claws that attach to your boots would be necessary to make it across the first section, a ramp of packed snow that went 300 feet up and into the base of the climb. The problem was, his crampons didn't fit his boots well. Unable to attach them to his feet with clips, he did what any MIT engineer would do—he used duct tape. I was stunned. Duct tape might be useful for a lot of things, but holding the spikes that would stop you from falling wasn't one of them.

I wasn't sure what to do. Mark insisted his "modified" crampons would hold, and I didn't know of any all-night mountaineering drive-throughs in the neighborhood. He reminded me that it was only 300 feet, and I relented.

I started up the first section with my tape-enhanced friend close behind. I got about halfway up through the snow when I could no longer hear him following. Not wanting to lose my temper, I didn't even look back. I figured he would catch up at the base, and I would have a moment to catch hold of myself. Then I heard him.

"Jeff, I, um, have a problem."

MountainVision

I turned around just in time to see one of his crampons sliding down over the frozen snow, surrounded by shredded pieces of tape. Without it, he wouldn't be able to continue up the short patch without assistance. I continued on to the base to attach a rope that I threw down to him. Along the way, I wondered very loudly what kind of idiot would use tape on his boots.

After nearly an hour of strenuous pulling, Mark finally joined me at the flat, rocky area from where we took the first rope climbing sections. We were already behind where I thought we should have been time-wise, and I wanted to make up ground. The first two pitches were simple enough, so I moved through them at a brisk pace, with Mark straining to imitate my performance. I was in a good rhythm by the time we reached the third, and more challenging pitch. Conversely, Mark seemed to be reaching his limit with every reach and step.

Within a few more minutes, our situation became painfully clear. About half way through the third pitch, I noticed the rope going tight, and then finding slack again. Mark was falling from one of his holds again and again. Due to the twist in the route, I was unable to see him. However, it was easy to tell from the taught nature of the rope what was taking place 100 feet below. The rope, fully extended, would go tight for longer and longer periods. I said nothing as I waited for him to regain his footing and make some progress, but eventually the rope stopped giving slack. Mark was stuck, and I was furious. I heard several incomprehensible bellows coming from below, until finally he admitted, "I can't do the move."

It was a real predicament. We were deep enough on Long's that there wasn't really a viable option to go back down. The same crooked notches and turns that were hiding Mark from my view made a retreat more difficult, and more dangerous, than climbing up had been. It was much simpler to get over the top and down the other side. I yelled this down to him, laying out my case in short sentences, but he couldn't get past his immediate dilemma. I went through the reasoning again. "Jeff, I just can't," was his only reply.

My temper erupted. "Can't is not a choice here, Mark! You wanted to do this damn climb, and now we have to do it!" There was no answer.

After a few minutes, Mark struggled through. As he pulled himself to my perch, I could see he was utterly exhausted and defeated. The effort had left him so spent he had to stop frequently, even through the short scrambling sections. Each time, I berated him for his poor effort. The afternoon came and went, but we trudged through into the next night. Eventually we did make it to the summit, and arrived back at our car 26 hours after we'd left it. I was exhausted, physically and mentally. What should have been an eight-hour climb had eaten more than an entire day.

As we settled into the seats, Mark tried to speak. He wanted to apologize for holding me back, but I wouldn't listen to his words. I cut him off, and then turned on the radio for the short drive home. As I dropped him at his house, I could see the wounded look on his face. But instead of staying to talk, I drove home for a nap.

After some sleep, I was able to get together with Mark over a beer and apologize to him. I had let my fatigue and impatience get the best of me. Being the great guy that he is, he forgave me right away and we've gone on as friends for years.

I'm ashamed to admit I let my mentor down that day. Mark looked to me to be his guide in that situation, just as I had looked to him to direct and support me so many times before. Being a leader isn't just about motivating people; it's also about knowing each person's abilities and limitations. I was in a unique position to judge whether Mark was ready to make that climb or not. When I decided he was, I should have made sure he was prepared and helped him through it. If he wasn't, I shouldn't have put him in a position to fail. Leadership is not based on a title or how many people answer to you. It's an attitude where you are constantly seeking out opportunities to lift your team up by showing your commitment to them and your shared goal.

MountainVision

At times, we're all put in leadership roles. Other people in our lives count on us for guidance and patience. Learn from my mistake and don't let them down.

CHAPTER 6

SOUTH AMERICA

As we searched for a new adventure, Erik and I realized that if we wanted to do something bigger, we'd have to start looking outside North America. While our native continent is blessed with several majestic strings of mountains—Erik and I had done peaks in the Alaska Range, the Cascades, the Sierras, and the Rockies—we wanted to try something farther beyond our backyard.

Aconcagua, the highest point in the western hemisphere, was a natural choice. Not only was the Argentinean giant the most famous in South America, it would be similar to Denali in both duration and elevation. It would be less difficult to climb than its northern cousin, but shared the same odd pressure characteristics because of its southerly orientation.

Following our ascent of El Capitan, we wanted to get back to big mountains and ride our momentum a bit. The American Foundation for the Blind was prepared to sponsor us on another trip, and we wanted to take the opportunity get out of our sandbox and generate some positive publicity for them. It seemed like things were getting easier for us. Whereas before we'd had to fight through miles of skepticism before anyone would take us seriously, now we had people ready to send us around the world with fresh new gear and provisions. Who were we to blow a chance like that?

As the trip neared, Chris, Erik, and I got together to re-acclimate ourselves with alpine conditions. We drudged our way up mountains in Colorado and California week after week, and soon we fell back into the rituals and routines that had served us so well in the past years. Over the long fall months, we threw ourselves into steep climbs and dreadful conditions, aware that we would see more of the same in South America.

The journey to Chile was long but engaging. For 17 hours I could barely sit or sleep as our flight drew nearer to Santiago. After we spent a couple of days getting acquainted with our South American colleagues, we departed on the eight-hour drive that would take us to the entrance of the mountain valley. From there, it was a three-day trek through the high alpine Andean landscape leading to base camp. In stark contrast to the base at Denali thriving with new arrivals, the first camp on Aconcagua was relatively empty. Although there were other groups on the mountain, most had taken the standard route. We were attempting a lesser-traveled option on the east side of the hill.

From base camp, I got my first glimpse of the mammoth we'd come all this way to stand upon. My immediate impression was that it wasn't pristine and beautiful, but that it held a striking, exotic quality. It rose like an upside-down "V" above the surrounding landscape, exerting its heavy influence on the forests and hills below. I had a strange feeling staring up into the wall of glaciers we'd eventually have to pass through. Every climber will tell you that each mountain has its own personality, and to me, Aconcagua seemed like an old movie mob boss—docile and generous from a distance, but belligerent and angry behind closed doors.

My intuition wasn't far off. The first few days offered sunny skies and light winds as we breezed through the lower altitudes. As we made our way into the higher camps, however, the sun dried up and gave over to light snow. Increasingly dark clouds gave birth to thunder, then lightning. The heavens were in a nasty mood, and it was getting worse. With each day of driving wind and snow, our spirits darkened. The farther we crawled, the more ferocious the wind became, whipping us with small stones and throwing dust in our eyes. Like the Chilean girls I'd met in town, the mountain seemed to have a blustery Latin temper, uninterested in entertaining American climbers.

The second week became the third as we neared high camp, the final resting point before we could attempt the summit. We spent our days sucking down oatmeal, which we also came to know as goat-meal, choke-meal, and bloat-meal, as we had on Denali, feeling certain the weather would break soon. At night, the wind reached speeds near 100 miles an hour, threatening to sweep us off the cliff.

We waited and waited. When our expedition had reached its 17th day, Chris informed me that he wanted to make a go at the summit. I agreed. As fearsome as the weather was, I couldn't bear the thought of coming all this way and not even trying to reach the summit. In the early hours, we set off into the cold. Even in the middle of the Chilean summer, the clouds threw down blankets of snow so thick we couldn't spread more than a few feet apart for fear we'd lose a member of the team. The morning wore on with no respite. Still, we kept hope alive as we made the way through our more sheltered pitches, hoping we could catch a break and steal a brief jaunt to the top.

A few hours after sunrise, we were at the point of no return. Ahead of us was a rocky bank that would lead to a couloir. The ice-packed channel extended up only a few hundred yards to the summit, but offered no protection from the elements. From our vantage point, it was clear the task would be insurmountable. It was unlikely any of us would survive the walk into what I could only describe as arctic tornado conditions, much less reach the summit.

We knew we had to go back, but still we deliberated. Shouting over one another through the deafening wind, we struggled to identify a way. It was obvious that a summit was out of the question, but we couldn't let go. Here we were, thousands of miles from home and 90 minutes from our goal. This was our only chance. Food and provisions, spent during the week of waiting for clearer skies, had been depleted. If we turned around now, our journey would end in failure.

MountainVision

In his wisdom, Chris said something at moment that I've always carried with me. Screaming to be heard, he looked at us one by one and shouted, "Reaching the summit is optional, but going home isn't." And with that, there was no more discussion, no more argument. We all knew he was right, and we could either live to face facts or die in a vain pursuit.

It had been a long time since we'd faced a defeat of this magnitude, and for a while I was angry. But as a few weeks passed, I came to realize that it just wasn't our time. Sometimes in life you set out to do something but you can't. It's hard when the reasons are out of your control, but it's just something to live with.

So much of our society expects success on every single level. We've made failure a taboo. It's easy to think we've lost because we weren't good enough or didn't try hard enough, but this is an illusion. In reality, a fall or setback is a needed event. Without it, we'd be complacent. What's important isn't avoiding failure, but using it as feedback. Cultivate an attitude in your mind, and an atmosphere in your team, that you're not afraid to come up short sometimes. Otherwise, the fear of failure will hold you back and keep you from venturing out and creating that vision. Fear will keep you on the couch.

After being beaten by the mountain on our first attempt, we regrouped a year later and went to the summit. It would have been easier if we'd made it up the first time, but we also wouldn't have learned anything. If you never fail, it means you're not testing yourself enough. It's better to put ourselves in situations where we may sometimes come up short and use those as a springboard for better things, than it is to stay in our comfort zone. You can make failure a habit or an excuse not to try, or you can make it work for you.

CHAPTER 7

RACING RUGGED

Gliding through the North Atlantic in a puny motorboat wasn't what I'd had in mind when we signed up to go to Greenland. Our captain would peek out at the choppy seas ahead to try and avoid the larger icebergs, and then whip his head back inside as the bitter cold bit into his face. Each time he ducked below, we could hear the hard whacks of ice chunks slamming against the hull. It would only take one good hit to sink us into the freezing water. I scanned the horizon for other boats, someone who might save us, but there were only rough waves and frozen blocks for miles.

We'd ended up in Greenland almost by accident. Just as Erik and I had begun to take our adventures outside of North America, we wanted to see if we could take them beyond climbing as well. We started to look for other ways to challenge ourselves while incorporating the skills we'd already learned. It had started out with a marathon in Cuba, followed by some longer rides on a tandem mountain bike. From that training, we began to embrace the idea of doing some adventure racing. The ultimate goal was to participate in Primal Quest, a sort of ultra-challenge that would include climbing, biking, kayaking, and other trekking skills.

After some long months of training in the Colorado backcountry, 24-hour periods of climbing several mountains followed by 100-mile bike rides, we felt ready to take on an actual race.

However, before we could enter, we'd need help. Each Primal Quest team needed to have four members. We'd have to find another pair who not only knew adventure, but were excited about the unique challenge of completing a race with Erik. We decided to partner with Rob and Cammy, two experienced racers who had approached us about entering a competition together.

After checking out some of the half-dozen races that would be held in the next few months, we decided we'd all like to see Greenland. Not only would the location be exotic, but the race would be longer and more demanding than many of the domestic

Kayaking in Greenland

competitions.

Our journey into the North Atlantic made me appreciate the genius of the Vikings. By giving Iceland and Greenland their respective names, they committed an advertising masterstroke and convinced many of their countrymen to bypass the smaller island and continue on. Our flight from Montreal had taken us into

Reykjavik, Iceland's breathtakingly beautiful capital. The country was lush, filled with green life and hot springs. The capital held a cosmopolitan feel with its clean streets and shining buildings.

Our arrival into Greenland was a stark contrast. Our suicidal speedboat journey deposited us into a sparse and barren land. A cold, biting wind gnawed into me as we unloaded our bags. The only signs of civilization were the short, metal-sided walls of the small collection of structures at the end of a muddy road. Iceland's old-world charm had been replaced by the kind of decor that most would associate with a Siberian prison camp.

Bleak as it was, it would still be a paradise for someone who likes the outdoors. The country is rugged and pristine, largely unfettered with roads, buildings, or any modern encumbrances. Greenland is the scenic equivalent of the Nordic women you see in the movies—strikingly beautiful, but also harsh and very unforgiving.

Only eight teams entered the competition. Most of the others were professionals, competing for sponsorship and prize money. We simply wanted to finish the race and get our bearings for Primal Quest.

The race began to wear us down immediately. The first day saw us summiting three different mountains. They were low, compared to the elevations we were used to in Colorado, rising only about 4,000 feet each. But they were hard-going, more like giant mounds of broken rock than actual peaks. For hours, we cut back and forth up loose surfaces, sinking and sliding with each step, to make our way to the top. After each grueling victory, we were left to hustle back down to sea level and take on another.

Worse than the terrain, I found almost immediately that I was becoming frustrated with Rob. As an experienced navigator, he poured over our maps to make sure we remained on course in the most direct routes. I was worried he wasn't taking Erik's needs into account. Several times we found ourselves mired in sections that were the shortest, by strict distance, but didn't make sense for the team. A straight line is not always the quickest route, especially with a blind team member. Without the benefits of my experience in guiding him, Rob kept sending us through areas that would be difficult for Erik, where we could have actually saved time by taking a longer route. I brought up my concerns, but he was convinced from his racing experience that we were moving efficiently.

The second day brought more climbing, followed by a long trek through several miles of rocky fields. After a couple hours of sleep, we broke camp and headed into a third day of hard mountain biking. The paths were sloppy and winding, punctuated with deep holes that threatened to drive us into the stones beneath us. For more than 15 hours, I steered frantically while shouting commands to Erik behind me. As I tore the handlebars right and left, he leaned his weight to one side or the other in tune with my directions. Every few minutes we'd go into a slide or a jarring bump I was sure was going to end with either a broken wrist or a concussion, but we made it through, barely, each time.

Racing across
Greenland

As the race progressed, I became more and more frustrated with Rob. Our tension was becoming palpable with each path he chose. He would calculate a path that seemed most direct from the map, whereas I would look ahead to the terrain and make a different assessment. We butted heads again and again, Rob wanting to take a direct route when I preferred another that seemed to take the same amount of time but spare us effort and frustration.

Finally, on the fifth morning we had a breakthrough. The team was roped together, climbing our way to the top of a glacier. We'd had a rough night, missing sleep to find our way through giant blocks of ice to catch up with the other teams. The sun edged its way over the peak we were moving toward, bathing the sea of ice around us in orange. The immense beauty of it seemed to affect us all, replacing our fatigue with a spirit of teamwork. At the top of the ridge, Rob called me over to look at the next section. A straight line would have led us through another field of crevasses that might have taken hours, but I noticed that by veering a few hundred yards we could save some time and effort. From there, Rob was able to plot a course leading us back by cutting through an outcropping that was barely visible to the eye, but clearly marked on the map. With that, things started clicking. We found that by looking at the tasks ahead together, we could get where we were going far more efficiently. We spent the rest of the morning moving through the barren countryside at a good clip. The whole team was in a great mood as we spotted the other teams' tents in the distance.

When we pulled into camp, we got some harsh news: we'd missed our cut-off time and been disqualified. Ultimately though, the loss didn't matter. Even though we failed to finish the race, we'd accomplished something bigger. We'd learned to work together. I had spent days thinking Rob was too busy with his head down, ignoring the reality in front of us. He was left wondering why I couldn't see what was being shown clearly on a map. It wasn't until we realized we were both looking at the same terrain but seeing it differently that we were able to function as a team.

As long as there are different people, there are going to be different ways of thinking and working. It's only natural; we're all good at different things. The trick is to pull together with those who are different than you and see if you can't complement each other's strengths. Sometimes the only thing you need to make it through the rough patches is a different perspective. Make a point of partnering up with someone who sees the world differently than you do, it might just take you off course and onto a better path.

CHAPTER 8

PRIMAL QUEST

I will always think of Primal Quest as my own personal nine-day tribute to suffering. The backcountry competition, formerly known as the Eco-Challenge, is infamous for the extreme strain it places on the human body and will, and we weren't disappointed. Erik, Rob, Cammy, and I were one of the hundred teams to enter the 460-mile race taking place around Lake Tahoe and the Sierra Nevada mountains. Although we'd been disqualified in Greenland, we were optimistic that we'd make a good showing.

The first morning started out well enough. We needed to navigate our way around Lake Tahoe in a pair of kayaks, successfully passing checkpoints laid out on the way. The setting was idyllic, with a serene dawn sky and water smooth as glass. We rowed at a good pace, each of us moving in synch with the other like a freshly tuned engine.

Our smooth launch was quickly interrupted. A few hours after daybreak, the wind picked up and the water beneath us unsettled itself. Our small boats drifted side-to-side as we tried to maintain a straight course. Our efforts were useless. The surface became more and more choppy until waves were rising above our heads and crashing down upon us. Erik and I paddled furiously just to keep the kayak from capsizing. It was hard to find any direction, much less speed. It was the first morning of a race that would take us over a week, and we were already fighting to survive; finding our way and finishing the race were secondary concerns by then. We simply worked our paddles into the angry water and hoped we were staying on course toward dry ground. Luckily, our path led us to shore in time to enter the next stage. Exhausted from six hours of trying not to drown, we crawled on to the next in a long string of horrors.

The remainder of the first day sent us on a run up Donner Pass, the site of the infamous, historic tragedy. Even in summer, the trail was cold and thick. As tiring as it was to climb uphill, I consoled myself with the fact that it was at least on dry ground. When we had finished the run, just after 1:00 a.m., we were rewarded with a mountain bike ride on the old Pony Express. The rocky trail had been somewhat preserved by off-road racers, but it wasn't in any shape for biking. Erik and I, trying to fight our way through the broken road on a tandem bike, weren't able to make the final stretch, a two-mile course that rose up sharply to a peak near the first camp. So, with Erik following behind me, I carried the nearly 50-pound bicycle on my shoulders. In that moment, it dawned on me quickly and clearly how stupid adventure racing was. It was to be the last lucid thought I'd have for nearly a week.

When we'd finally reached the peak, we could see other teams ahead of us. Relieved, we decided to follow them into the first checkpoint. After a half-mile jaunt through the rough terrain on the other side of the hill we pulled up to a camp ... or so we thought. We'd expected a collection of tents and the trailer that our support team packed with food and supplies. As bad as the first day had been, at least some warm food and a few hours' rest were in order. Instead, what we found was a collection of a couple of dozen racers scattered around the area, most of them lying on the open ground. I walked to the closest, a young woman sitting with her face in her hands. I could hear her weeping, and when I asked what was wrong she simply pointed ahead. I took a few more steps and then understood her pain. Where the camp should have been, there was only a tall barbed wire fence. They'd gotten lost, and we'd followed them.

Worse than being lost was realizing the only way out was back up the hill we'd just come down. Our team was too tired to even move, much less carry bikes uphill for an hour or more. We quickly huddled up and made the decision, as the other teams had, to simply spend the night at this spot and pick it up again in the morning. There was no room for sleeping bags while we were biking, so our only protection from the elements were the small foil blankets we'd brought for emergencies.

The four of us, tucked into the metallic sheets that looked like pop tart wrappers, arranged ourselves into a small dog pile. We were 7,000 or 8,000 feet up, all of us in wet Lycra, and the night air was biting. So, for the first (and hopefully last) time, I spooned a grown man. Between Erik and me, there is an ongoing debate on who spooned whom. Aside from the uncomfortable questions about my sexuality, the warmth allowed us to get a solid 90 minutes of sleep before we'd have to get up and race again.

After the nap, we woke as the sun was cresting over the surrounding peaks. Ninety minutes wasn't much time to sleep, but it gave us a chance to gather our strength for the sunrise assault. As we rose into the frosty morning, the only way to keep warm was to charge up the hill we'd put off with the bike on my back. Two hours later we rolled into camp to prepare for the next stage.

The second and third days were all about biking. At first, we took the tandem through heavily forested alpine trails. Those eventually turned into actual backcountry roads, which we followed for more than a hundred miles.

While the pavement was a welcome change, the lack of sleep was beginning to have profound effects on our minds and bodies. I was the first to begin hallucinating, seeing gnomes and elves that would scurry beside the road and hide behind trees. This was followed by images of snakes slithering across the trail. I knew they couldn't really be there, but still I was petrified they'd bite me if I stepped or rode on top of them. I wasn't alone in my delusions. Erik was conjuring up memories of his fifth grade class, urging him on and telling him he couldn't quit. I found out later that hallucinations are a common part of the struggle for adventure racers.

MountainVision

Seeing things was only the beginning. It quickly became clear why sleep deprivation is used as a form of torture. My head pounded and felt constantly light as we went on and on. We'd stocked ourselves with enough caffeine drinks to last a year, but they weren't helping. Each sip seemed more of an effort to get to our mouths than it rewarded in extra fuel. Erik and I had resorted to heavy tactics to keep each other awake. We'd run through all of the jokes we knew, talked about the race and mountains we'd been on, and finally, just punched each other to stay awake.

After one such pounding in the back, Erik had been telling me some stories from his school. We were making good time, doing 40 miles per hour down a paved stretch. At one point, he got quiet and I wondered if he was choked up thinking about his students.

I tried to reassure him. "It's okay man, let it go." Still there was no answer. "Erik?" He didn't reply.

Without further warning, the bike lurched to the left. It was almost as if 170 pounds of dead weight had tilted to one side. I started screaming at Erik as loudly as I could. After a few shouts the bike lurched again, this time to the right.

"Did you just fall asleep at forty miles per hour?" I screamed at him.

"I guess so," he replied.

His nap had nearly killed us, causing our flimsy tandem bike to jump left and then right at high speed, but I couldn't be upset. I was on the edge of collapse myself, terrified I'd nod off and send us into a neck-breaking accident. Luckily, rest wasn't far off. We got to camp twenty minutes later for an hour of deep sleep.

The fifth day brought an orienteering course. With nothing more than a map and our sleep-deprived brains, we had to navigate ourselves to a flag buried dozens of miles into some wild bush country. The hike was pure misery, punctuated by a run-in with a wasps' nest and an impromptu hug with a poison ivy bush. Our team was starting to look a bit ragged, and I was wondering if we would make it to our checkpoints in time. With only a few minutes to spare, we pulled into camp on the sixth morning for an hour's rest.

Jeff Evans

We were preparing for the next day's segment, whitewater rafting, when medical problems began to appear. For days we had been drinking lots of Gatorade rather than water. The sugar from the drink, sitting in our dry mouths, was beginning to form painful ulcers. Erik's feet were bleeding, Cammy was looking at a sprained ankle, and I had poison ivy in my Fruit of the Looms.

Still, we knew we only had to make it two more days, and we were determined to finish. After a short rest, we threw ourselves into the river for a whitewater rafting trial. Rob, who was a stronger paddler, got in a boat with Erik, while I got in with Cammy. Then, we set off for the five-hour trip down river.

It was during the whitewater section that fatigue nearly killed me. We had already made our way through the more difficult parts of the rush and I had become complacent. As Cammy and I worked our way through and around the rapids, our small kayak got stuck against two rocks. We were lodged sideway against the stones, with about three feet between them. Wanting to free the boat, I put one leg out on the upriver side taking a moment to note the shallow water, but moving quickly. The kayak was firmly pinned against the rocks. Without thinking, I put my other leg out on the same side and almost immediately after my foot touched the rushing water the force of the tide swept my legs right out from under me. I hung on from under the boat, my chest barely above water. Cammy threw her hand out to stop me from being dragged under, but wasn't able to support my weight against the tide.

I didn't know what was on the other side of the boat hidden beneath the water, but I wasn't eager to find out. There could be an opening, but there could just as easily have been another stone that I'd smash my head against. I struggled for several seconds, trying desperately to pull myself back up into the boat, but I was falling farther underneath, and I knew it.

Finally, my hands slipped off the side of the boat and I was dragged under. The second or two it took me to pass through the water seemed like an eternity. A million thoughts passed through my mind, and yet it was also completely still. When I came out through the other side there was no rock, only an open space in the water. I was able to crawl to my feet and dislodge the boat.

As anyone who has narrowly escaped death can tell you, the feeling is beyond description. In that moment, my fatigue melted away and I was overcome with joy. I felt such gratitude to be alive and able to have the experience of the race.

At last, we reached the last stage of the competition, another row through Lake Tahoe. Cold and numb, we climbed into the small watercraft and began to make our way through the water in the dark.

We were nearly finished, the feeling of relief beginning to wash over us, when we saw lights in the distance, both ahead and behind. The end of the course was a half-mile ahead, but a couple-hundred yards behind us were the boats of another team. We hadn't seen another party for several hours, believing the teams behind us had all been disqualified. But here was one more, and they were trying

Jeff and the team at the finish line of Primal Quest

to catch us.

Rob, Cammy, Erik, and I looked at each other; no words were needed. After nine days of suffering, we were not going to finish last. We picked up our paddling, but the other boat still gained. They were clearly in a mad dash, as we were, not to be the final finishers. Our arms and shoulders were rubbery and enflamed, but still we tore into the water with every last ounce of strength we could find. When we reached the shore, the other team was no more than a hundred yards behind us.

We wept like children, overcome with fatigue and elation in our small win. After sixteen hours of sleep in nine days, I worried we might collapse on the spot, but we managed to hold on a few minutes to congratulate each other and the other final competitors.

I think Primal Quest was a major point of growth for us, even though it might not seem that way to the outside world. After all, we didn't win a single thing. We'd finished nearly dead last and taken almost twice as long as the winning team. But we did press ourselves to the absolute edge of exhaustion, and still found the will to compete. We'd come to prove we could finish, and we did.

CHAPTER 9

THINKING BIG

The idea of climbing Mount Everest came to us slowly. In the years after we finally defeated Aconcagua, we kept looking around the globe for new challenges. We didn't have a checklist or a specific dream we were looking to fulfill, we just never felt like we were finished. Along the way, we'd picked up the idea of finishing the seven summits, the highest points on each of the continents. In addition to Denali and Aconcagua, we'd completed Kilimanjaro in Tanzania and Elbrus in Russia. There was one glaring exception,

Mt Everest, 29,035 ft.

which happened to be the highest in the world.

Jeff Evans

Erik and I got together in May of 2000 to try and find the next adventure. We both agreed we'd accomplished some big things, but now we wanted to do something outrageous, something no one thought we could finish. This time, there was no doubt as to where we'd go. There was only one place, one peak, one summit that would satisfy us—Everest.

Of course we were familiar with the mountain. As climbers we'd read all the books and seen all the movies. We had friends and acquaintances who'd tried the mountain and even a few that had made it to the top. But could we realistically give it a go?

We poured ourselves into the task of learning more about it. We talked about all the technical and logistical difficulties we'd face, along with problems we probably hadn't even thought of that were bound to pop up. In the end, we decided we wouldn't be able to forgive ourselves if we didn't at least give it a try.

To embark upon an Everest expedition is a massively expensive undertaking. Flights, gear, Sherpa assistance, and especially permits from the Nepali government are all heavy costs. Just to get there and back would cost more than most families spend on a home. We knew that in order to raise the kind of sponsorship money we'd need; we'd have to go public with our goal. We also knew the moment we did, there would be no shortage of people telling us it was a bad idea, and we weren't disappointed.

Within a matter of days, a small army of outspoken doubters came out of the woodwork. Many well-known Everest experts went on the record saying it was foolish and dangerous to try to take a blind man to the world's highest point. Many suggested, either subtly or directly, that Erik would almost certainly die, and possibly the rest of the team as well. They said we didn't realize what we were in for and, while we'd had some success, this would be impossible. They pointed out most sighted climbers couldn't make it to the top. They went on and on, publicly and privately. Erik and I must have heard a thousand reasons why it wouldn't work. We listened to their concerns, but we didn't agree. After all we'd been through together, there just wasn't room for their disbelief. They were experts on Everest, but they weren't experts on us.

Because we believed in ourselves, we found others who believed in us, too. It began with our families and friends, who pitched in from the start with emotional support and encouragement. From there, it spread to others who heard about our ambitions. One by one, climbers signed on to be a part of our team. Major sponsors, some of whom had never worked with us before, lined up behind us. Many had never funded a climbing expedition, but they pledged their money to help us do the impossible.

In the end, I think the support we got from everyone who helped us was worth much more than the money and gear they gave. We didn't want to rest on our past success. To go further and higher, we needed to surround ourselves with people who weren't afraid to do something that seemed impossible. They shared our vision to send a blind man to the top of the world. We'd set a huge goal for ourselves, and if we were going to fail, it was going to be on the way to the top of the world, not at home thinking about it.

The journey into Nepal was an adventurer's dream. After our flight from Kathmandu, we took the weeklong trek through the beautiful high countryside and small villages leading to Everest base camp. Worn trails and stone paths led us across rolling hills and sloping valleys, with the Himalayan peaks looking down at us all the while. As we became accustomed to the Central Asian alpine scenery, we learned about its inhabitants as well. The people we met were every bit as proud and captivating as the mountains surrounding them. At every stop, we were greeted with smiling faces and warm hugs. Families who had little to share, heartily invited us into their homes. Everyone we met was eager to help or make a friend, even though they expected nothing in return.

The base camp itself was not unlike the sites we'd been through on other mountains around the world, except everything was bigger. The three-month haul up the mountain required a small army of support, along with tons of gear. In any given season, there might be 50 or more teams trying to make their way up the mountain, each consisting of anywhere from 5 to 25 people. Base camp, sitting at 17,000 feet, is where all those people and their equipment come together in a sprawling collection of tents and piles.

There were parties from every corner of the globe. Some were experienced climbers who had saved for a shot at their holy grail. Others were wealthy adventurers who had purchased the best gear and help money could buy in hopes of finding a way to the top. No matter their background, everyone was keenly aware of the excitement and danger that lurked in the weeks ahead. Everest was a place where you could find glory or die trying, and scores of people each climbing season did.

While the mountain is popular with the public and the media, (a simple web search will yield hundreds of books, articles and movies), few people appreciate how difficult it actually is to climb. During the three-month undertaking, you don't just go up once. In fact, through a series of ascents and descents to and from the camps on the route, you actually have to go up and down the lower sections of Everest about five times. This is partly because of your gear. All of the oxygen canisters, coats, ice axes, and other implements required for a shot at the summit must be moved by foot from base camp to the top. This represents literally tons of equipment for each person, and, at the risk of stating the blatantly obvious, moving it uphill through fields of ice at high altitude is no easy task.

More importantly, however, is the need to acclimatize. The body just can't function at such a high altitude without taking some time to adjust. Consider this: If you could be flown by helicopter to the summit of Everest right this second, with all the best equipment at your side, you'd still be unconscious within five minutes, and dead within ten. Not due to the frigid temperatures, but rather because the oxygen is so thin your brain would swell in a matter of moments.

MountainVision

Even at base camp, which is higher than many of the greatest mountains outside the Himalayas, it's not uncommon to see headaches, vomiting, and other effects of altitude sickness. It's only by taking months moving into and out of the camps, inching your way up the mountain, that you can give your body a fighting chance at surviving to see the top.

Beyond the problems of air and altitude, Everest carries the same weather and terrain dangers as any other high-altitude peak. Blizzards, avalanches, and falling rocks kill climbers each year. Assorted illnesses and falls routinely claim victims as well. It's understood when you set off from base camp that the best you can do is look out for the obvious dangers, and then pray that you'll be alright.

In that department, we were open to any help we could get. Nearly every team that passes through base camp stops to see the monks who hold a blessing ceremony for climbers on their way up. We had the good fortune of passing through at a time when a Rinpoche, a high-ranking Buddhist religious figure, was milling about. He was exactly the way you'd picture a monk should be. At about four feet tall with heavily lined dark skin and a heavy accent, he looked like an earthly Yoda in his saffron robes. At our request, he agreed to perform the blessing personally.

After we'd all gathered, the Rinpoche offered us what we came to learn were the prerequisites for praying—Russian vodka and Chinese whiskey. Once we had all imbibed, he read from a copy of the Tibetan Book of Prayers that appeared to have predated fire. It had a sort of leather covering and ancient pages held together with a kind of yarn. We arranged ourselves and our climbing gear in a circle around a chorten, a small pile of rocks in the center. For over an hour he rumbled the passages in low tones, more of a chant than a recital, dabbing each of us and our equipment with yak butter.

When he had finished blessing our expedition, he went around to each of us to offer words of good fortune and encouragement. In the dim light from the tent fire, and with nearly two dozen of us in the room, he hadn't realized Erik was blind, and no one had told him.

Jeff Evans

As he placed his hand out to shake hands, Erik felt out in front of him and offered his hand at an angle away from the small monk. The Rinpoche turned to me with a confused look, forced a pained smile, and in his broken English asked, "he also going?"

When we explained about our blind friend, the Rinpoche became quiet. After a moment of contemplating, he asked us each for an empty film canister, which we produced. He disappeared momentarily, and then returned with the canisters. Each had been filled with dried rice he had blessed. He instructed us to take the canisters with us, and toss a pinch of the rice into the wind as an offering any time we felt particularly frightened or endangered.

I remember thinking to myself, we're on Everest, how would I know when that would be?

Just beyond base camp lies Everest's first major challenge, as well as one of its most deadly. The Khumbu Ice Fall is a large glacier field with huge crevasses cut into its floor that descend thousands of feet down, and sometimes more. A jumbled mess of chaos running about a mile long and sloping upward a few thousand feet, its traps shift daily as glaciers burn and expand under the sun. Passing through is extremely treacherous, a thought that never leaves your mind as the frozen columns groan and crack around you. The only way through is by stepping over a series of aluminum ladders that have been roped together as makeshift bridges to carry you over the dark pits. The Sherpas liked to tell us that if we fell, the crevasses were so deep that we'd end up back in America. I wasn't inclined to doubt them. There are a thousand ways to die in Khumbu; falling is only the most terrifying of them.

Everyone we'd spoken to had stressed the importance of moving through the Ice Fall as quickly as possible, and I could see why. The longer you were there, the bigger the risk that a chunk of ice would break off from one of the surrounding walls and crush you or that the ground would shift and you'd be swallowed by a deep crevasse.

Worse still was the psychological effect. Simply put, the Ice Fall terrorized your mind. As I made my way across the first series of ladders, which swayed and moved under my weight, my heart rendered most of my body numb. The only thing keeping me from a freefall into the endless, dark oblivion below were a few discount ladders tied together by some sort of Sherpa Kmart boat twine. A kind of minor panic set in with each step, until I reached the end of a pit, only to feel a moment's relief before facing the next one.

Things were going slowly, but I was making progress. Until I reached the long crevasse bridged by six ladders, that is. One or two had been tolerable, but this was sheer insanity. It stretched on and on, the middle ladders sagging noticeably downward. I told my legs to keep going forward, but my body refused to move. I finally took the first step, only to watch the ladder at the far end jolt and slide. I closed my eyes and tried to regain my calm, taking one small rung at a time under my feet. The flimsy support below me was still gliding right to left as sweat poured down into my eyes.

In my fear, I did the worst thing you can ever do in the Ice Fall—I looked down.

What I saw wasn't nothing, it was worse than that. The sheer blackness extended down forever, and it seemed to be drawing me closer. I could feel it wanting to swallow me, like the frozen gateway to an icy hell. There was no sound, no movement or expression, only its unrelenting pull. Paralyzed, I thought of my pinch of rice. Moving slowly so as not to upset the balance below me, I carefully took the film canister from the side pocket where I'd stowed it and dumped every last grain into the pit. We all had a good laugh, and I was able to pull myself together.

Having gotten past my terror, I was able to regain my focus and work my way to the far end and onto solid ice. With each section completed, I had to turn and try to calmly guide Erik across verbally. I had explained to him what we'd be crossing and the dire consequences if he got it wrong. Watching him from a dozen yards away, every step was nerve-racking.

Holding onto ropes for guidance and feeling the edges of the ladders beneath him to make out his steps, Erik made his way over the crevasses. I was surprised at his strong progress, until he came to the middle of a long section and stopped. The ice around us had been groaning from the punishment offered by the afternoon sun. I was worried my friend was suffering from the same brand of terror that I had, and I wanted to comfort him.

In the calmest voice I could muster, I asked "Are you scared?"

Erik paused and put on his most thoughtful expression. "I'm fine, but I'm not sure this construction would be in compliance with the Americans with Disabilities Act."

Erik flashed a big grin and I broke out laughing in spite of myself. How could he be making jokes at a time like this? Later, I found out the secret to Erik's quick progress in the Ice Fall. Because he couldn't see, he didn't have the temptation to look down and be distracted by the fear of falling. For him, the ladders were just like any other place on Everest, or any other mountain for that matter. He had to focus and concentrate on each step, or he wouldn't make it. There was no room in his attention for what would come before or after that, only the immediate task in front of him.

Jeff guiding Erik through the ice fall.

Over the next few months, we shuttled through the ice fall more than a dozen times. It was never easy, but I had learned my lesson from Erik's example after that first crossing and it served me well on

MountainVision

Everest, and afterward, in life. Taking on any large project, like climbing Mount Everest, can seem overwhelming. The way to get through it is to focus on what's in front of you and celebrate the minor victories. See the big picture, know why you're doing what you're doing, but don't let that keep you from moving forward. The only way to beat a large mountain is with millions of small steps.

Standing next to Everest, and connected to it, is the Lhotse Shar. The world's fourth highest mountain, Lhotse is a mammoth in its own right and would be a major climbing destination in any other setting. As it is, anyone looking to scale Everest via the traditional routes has to spend a significant amount of time making their way across Lhotse in order to make a summit attempt on its taller sister. The mountain's western flank is known as the Lhotse Face. With nearly 4,000 feet of glacial blue ice extending to the South Col of Everest, the Face is an extremely dangerous place to be. Along with the usual dangers of altitude, its heavy slope—ranging from fifty degrees to completely vertical—means that objects like rocks can come falling down at any time.

A few years ago, an experienced climber was making his way up the Lhotse Face. He was doing everything right, not taking any careless chances or pushing himself too hard or too quickly. Reaching his arm up for the next grip, he saw a small dot coming down at him. He wasn't able to get out the way quickly enough and the object hit him in the chest. What he had thought was a small stone had bounced off him and finally come to rest in a pile of snow a few feet below. The object wasn't a stone at all, but a Snickers bar someone had dropped out of their bag from a few-hundred feet above him. Frozen through from the extreme cold, the candy bar had become the equivalent of a brick dropped from 30 or 40 stories above.

Jeff Evans

The hard thud of the impact seemed to knock the wind out of him. Unable to find his breath, he halted his ascent and waited for help. When his climbing partners reached him, they found him wheezing and struggling to get his words out. By feeling under his jacket and listening to his breath, his teammates were able to figure out that the candy bar had broken two of his ribs, causing one to puncture his lung.

Knowing they would have to act quickly to get help, they decided to evacuate the climber down. By the time he reached camp a few hours later, however, he was losing consciousness. That night, he died.

His story is unfortunate, but not as unusual as you might think. On a mountain, there are a thousand things that can get you at any moment. Falls, weather, and even the occasional rogue snack can do you in. It's dangerous, but I also think it makes climbers fortunate in a way. It makes us realize how fragile life is, and how quickly everything you have can be gone in the blink of an eye. We appreciate our families, our homes, our jobs so much more because we've all come too close to losing them.

I know most people will never climb a huge mountain—they're too smart for that. They might think Everest is a dangerous place, and he had it coming just for being there. They might be right. But don't fool yourself into thinking that things only happen on mountains. Take the time to appreciate your family, your friends, and your life. You never know where your chocolate bar might be falling from.

On our own journey up the Lhotse Face, Erik and I labored through seven hours of intense exhaustion. Despite our fatigue, however, we were in great spirits. The sky was clear, and we were nearing our attempt on the Everest summit. It was hard to believe our great luck.

MountainVision

Lhotse is known for massive storms but we were sneaking through on a clear morning ... or so we thought.

About half an hour from the end of the last pitch, I stopped to take a few pictures of the face. Through the camera's view, I could make out a small cloud creeping in from above. It looked to be nothing more than a speck, but I couldn't believe how quickly it was moving. The combination of high alpine terrain, the heavy summer sun, and jet stream force winds at that altitude means that weather or wind might be going over 70 or 80 miles per hour. Aware of how quickly things could change in the Himalayas, I immediately called to Erik to stop what he was doing and brace himself.

Working in a mad scramble, we dug out any protection that we could and roped ourselves into the line. Thirty seconds later, our clear skies had been replaced by a pounding storm. It had taken half a minute to go from a clear day into a heavy alpine blizzard, complete with pounding snow and nearly tornado-force winds. Those few moments were all the warning we received to recognize the changing situation and prepare for it.

As we went on, we learned to recognize and anticipate Everest's mood swings. No matter what you were doing or where you were, you had to be prepared for a tempestuous storm at any time. One of the key elements of success for us, and probably any other team for that matter, was flexibility, the ability to be ready to change and adapt. Directions change, plans change, life changes. Make yourself ready, because the job or the life you have right now probably won't be the same for long. Keep your eye on the ridge, watch for the weather, and be prepared.

Babu Chiri Sherpa was the undisputed reigning champ on Everest. Not only had he reached the summit ten times, but he had also set the mind-staggering speed record from base camp to summit in 16 hours. In another display of raw human skill, he'd become the first climber to intentionally spend the night at the top of the mountain, a good 3,000 feet into the death zone.

His success on the mountain had granted him fame in his home country of Nepal, as well as with climbers around the world, so I was excited to get the chance to meet him during our first week at Everest base camp. All the teams had gathered for a kind of orientation dinner as a brief chance to see and meet the parties with whom we'd be sharing the mountain. Two things about this man struck me immediately. The first was that he was genuinely kind and soft-spoken. You'd never have known from his humble, generous attitude that he was a mountaineering celebrity. The second thing I noticed right away was he was fat. He certainly wasn't obese, but it was clear the iron man I'd always pictured as a kind of tenacious bear could put away the groceries.

I didn't see Babu again until several weeks later. Our team was spending the night at Camp II, but I hadn't been feeling well. The weather was good, so I decided to make my way down to base camp to spend a day of rest regaining some strength at the lower elevation. As I made my way through the ice fall, I came upon a pair who were making their way down, but seemed to be struggling.

When I reached them I was able to make out Babu as the first climber. He had a short rope attached to his waist extending only a few feet away to a climber behind him. He seemed to be using the rope's tension, along with verbal commands to guide the second man. They weren't making quick progress. I caught up with them quickly, and Babu explained his predicament.

The second climber, Babu's client, had cerebral edema, an excess of fluid in the brain that can be brought on by altitude sickness. It is not uncommon on Everest, but it can be deadly. Among its many symptoms—headaches, hallucinations, and loss of coordination—the condition can also lead to temporary blindness. This man had lost his sight higher up, and now Babu was trying to help him back down through the Ice Fall to the safety of base camp.

I couldn't believe the coincidence. In a thousand years, I wouldn't have been able to dream up a situation in which Babu could use my help on Everest. He had forgotten more about mountaineering than I'd ever learn. But here he was, trying to guide a blind man through the Ice Fall. This was a topic I knew something about.

After quickly explaining this to Babu, we rearranged ourselves to guide the man across the maze of ladders and crevasses that stood between us and safer ground. Using the techniques I'd honed over my years working with Erik, we were able to reach base camp only a couple of hours later. Once we'd arrived, both Babu and his client thanked me profusely. I explained it had been my privilege to help, and then headed to our team's area for some rest.

The next morning, Babu sought me out in my tent, asking if he could show his gratitude more formally by inviting me to his mess tent in base camp for Sherpa tea and cookies. I didn't feel as though any additional thanks were needed, but I wasn't going to pass up the chance to spend a couple of hours with climbing royalty. I cheerfully accepted, and we made our way to his tent.

For two hours, Babu and I traded climbing stories and details of our lives. True to his humble nature, he insisted on calling me "Mr. Jeff," and continually insisted I have more cookies than would be polite for me to accept. As when we'd first met, I was truly in awe of the man, not only because of the spectacular feats he had accomplished in the Himalayas, but also because he managed to hold himself with such grace and integrity. As we parted ways, I tried to impress upon him what an honor it had been to have shared in his time. I walked away beaming, knowing I had a memory I'd always treasure.

Three days later, I got the news that Babu had died. He was settled in with his clients at Camp II, a relatively safe area of the mountain. Like anywhere else on Everest, it has its dangers, but the area was mostly flat, with small, easily avoidable crevasses. As the story went, he decided to step out of his tent at dusk and take a few photos for his family. He had backed up a couple of feet to get a wider angle, and slipped into a hole. Babu fell ninety feet, landing on his head and dying instantly.

I was shocked by the news, as was his country. Babu was more than a climbing icon; he was a great man in every sense of the word. It seemed impossible he could have been killed in a comparatively safe area of the mountain on a clear day. But that is the nature of mountaineering, and the way of life. No matter who you are and what you've done, you can never decide you're going to take it easy. Those moments in our lives and careers when we think we've got it made are often the deadliest, when our confidence can do away with us. I learned two great things from Babu: that a great man can be humble, and that, even after 10,000 right steps, you can't afford a wrong one.

In the months after we'd made our first trip through the Ice Fall, we continued our slow crawl up Everest, moving ourselves and our gear from camp to camp up the mountain and back down again. The repeated hauls from base camp wore on endlessly until our arrival at Camp III weeks later, but they would prepare our bodies and equipment for a summit assault.

Camp III itself was little more than a semi-flat area carved out on the side of a glacier. Blustery and freezing at over 24,000 feet, it was a miserable place to sleep. There's nothing but ice below you, and the wind rips at you viciously through the night. Worst of all, however, was the snow drifting down the side of the mountain. As strong gusts whipped the tent, small pockets of powder would fill in beneath the floor, tilting it up and threatening to slide us off a cliff and into oblivion.

Luckily, we only spent one sleepless night before moving on. When early morning arrived, we were all anxious to leave behind Camp III and its nightmarish elements for the real dangers higher up. With every increase in elevation, the altitude becomes more and more treacherous. Out of the hundreds of people who have died on the mountain, most have been at the top tiers. High winds clear the snow, leaving only ice and loose rocks for footing. It's easier to slip and fall, and the consequences for doing so are more severe. To make matters worse, your oxygen-starved brain starts making bad decisions. In a place where you can't afford a single mental error, you're reduced to the brainpower of a yak by the lack of air.

To somewhat mitigate this problem, we began taking oxygen from canisters, coming out of Camp III. Doing this didn't restore our air to what it would be like at sea level, but at least it did give us that extra bit of breathable gas that could make the difference.

Among Everest fanatics, there has long been a debate over whether using supplemental oxygen on the mountain is sporting. The first groups to summit in the fifties used oxygen, as do most modern teams. Still, there are some groups of climbers who consider using oxygen to be "cheating." Mountaineers, they feel, should rely on their own physical assets, and nothing more, to make their ascents. Our team had discussed this, but we agreed almost immediately we wanted to use every tool we had at our disposal to increase our chances of success. For me, it was never an issue. I wouldn't think of going up Everest without oxygen any more than I would think about climbing it barefoot. The air was a valuable tool that helped me stay alive, and I was glad for it.

Shortly out of camp, we moved up across angular, rocky growth called the Yellow Band and another called the Geneva Spur. It was a long day of climbing, but even in my exhaustion I couldn't help but marvel at the beauty of it. They weren't the kinds of spectacular views you'd see on a postcard, but the simple fact that they were so close to the highest summit on earth made them captivating. As the day wore on, I tried to savor the experience and take in everything I could before we finally settled in for the evening. It occurred to me that I might never see these places again after we left the mountain. But my thoughts turned as we reached our destination for the day. Things were serious now—Camp IV and the 8,000-meter death zone.

The death zone isn't a mysterious or dramatic climbing name, it's a simple reminder of where you are. At 8,000 meters, or about

26,000 feet, the human body has a hard time finding or extracting oxygen from the atmosphere. At one-third the air pressure you'd find at sea level, there just isn't enough oxygen to go around. As a result, lots of bad things start to happen.

Obviously, it gets hard to breath. Climbing uphill feels like you're running a marathon while breathing through a straw. Vomiting and diarrhea are normal occurrences. Sleep is hard to find, while pounding headaches are not. Typically, a person won't feel hungry or thirsty, which is just as well because the stomach can't absorb any nutrition from the food you consume, so it just goes right through you. The body does still need protein, however, so it begins to break down muscle tissue in an effort to cannibalize itself.

Topping everything off is the cold, which is extreme even by alpine standards. Any piece of exposed skin will pick up frostbite. Hands and feet are vulnerable as well, meaning that even those who make the summit often pay with missing fingers and toes. In short, at 8,000 meters you're dying quickly, and the only thing you can do to stop it is leave.

We arrived at Camp IV in the afternoon, with the intention of leaving for the summit at night. If the weather cooperated, we'd climb through the evening and arrive at the summit just after daybreak. However, when the whole team had finally arrived and gotten settled, it became obvious we weren't all going to be ready. A few of us could probably have made a successful attempt, but as a whole, the group was too tired and ragged. We'd come all that way and we had to make a difficult choice: either some of us could push through and try to summit, or we could risk taking a night at Camp IV and hope that all, or any, of us could make it with an extra day's rest.

It was late May, near the end of climbing season. In a few days, the Sherpas below would pull down the ladders that made traversing the Ice Fall possible. After that, a return to Camp IV would not be possible. And even if it were, we didn't have the supplies or the strength for another go at it. There was only going to be one shot.

MountainVision

After all the time spent training and preparing, tens of thousands of dollars invested, and 10 weeks on the mountain, I expected a heated argument between those who felt they could make it and those who were too exhausted. To my surprise, however, there was no conflict. After we'd gotten into our tents and opened the conversation via radio, we went around one by one to determine each climber's readiness. It quickly became apparent we couldn't all go on, so the team decided to stay another day, with no discussion of splitting up or leaving anyone behind. We decided that if we could make a summit attempt after a night in the death zone, that would be wonderful. But if we couldn't, we'd be able to say we came and left as a team.

For 24 hours, we milled around, trying to save whatever strength we could while our bodies ate at themselves. We passed the time by trying to sleep and or play cards in our tents. Even with a Braille deck, it's normally not that difficult to beat Erik at a game of poker. Usually a slight lean is all it takes to figure out if he's bluffing or not. With oxygen masks on, however, my cheating was accompanied by a Darth Vader sound effect. Again and again, I'd maneuver for a closer look, only to find my snooping met with a hard punch to the chest. As we played, blustery storms slapped at the sides of our tent. It sounded as if the world was going to hell outside our nylon walls, but we tried to keep it out of our minds.

I woke on the second night, minutes before the alarm was set to go off. It was pitch black, and there was no sound except the wind slapping away at the walls of our tent. Slowly, I sat up and turned on my headlamp. One by one, my teammates did the same. Everyone began waking up and getting equipment in order, but no one spoke. Our small tent was like a locker room on Super Bowl Sunday. We were in for the biggest day of our climbing lives and we all knew it. Except for a few nearly hidden smirks, no one wanted to acknowledge or jinx the moment.

In the near darkness, we set about the work of getting our packs together. We knew we'd be away from camp for at least 24 hours, moving to even higher and more dangerous ground. We had to be absolutely sure we had anything and everything we might need, and knew where to find it. We packed and checked again and again, knowing anything forgotten might cost a life.

With everything we expected to need stowed into place, we stepped outside the tent and into the wind tunnel outside. We gathered together for one last count, and any final thoughts or instructions. After some of the team gave a few thoughts on the weather and some notes of encouragement, Erik stepped forward. I thought he was going to offer profound words of wisdom, or perhaps say something motivational to the team, but instead he did something better—he pulled aside his oxygen mask and puked.

Some people might have considered this to be a bad omen, especially at that altitude, but I was elated. Over the years, I'd come to see Erik's vomit as a sign of good fortune to come. On every major mountain we'd gone up together—Denali, Aconcagua, Rainier, and others—a successful summit had been preceded by my blind friend emptying his stomach. I never knew why he did it, but I knew what it meant. It was time to get him to the top.

We filed out one by one into the darkness, leaving Camp IV behind. The sense of anticipation and nervousness that had been with us as we made our preparations soon melted into the hours of trudging up steep snow slopes and across rocky bulges. The wind beat down on us, but we moved efficiently, following each step with a few resting breaths. The object was to keep making progress upward through the packed snow and ice surface below, while holding on to enough strength to see the night through.

Even though our whole team was in a line moving upward, the setting was intensely isolating. The only thing I could see was the small pocket of light immediately in front of me provided by my headlamp, past that it seemed like the rest of the world had gone away. I found myself lost in my own thoughts, Erik trudging along happily behind me in some of his favorite terrain.

It was as we were packing our equipment that I first noticed a strong sensation in my chest. It was hardly noticeable at first, but as we made our final preparations and set off into the cold night, it grew stronger. It wasn't a pain, but a tingle that was welling up inside me. With my medical training, I knew the cardiovascular risks we'd taken by being at altitude so long, but I didn't feel afraid. The sensation wasn't hurting me, it felt more like it was giving me strength. Now, making our way over the ice bulge, I could feel it increasing. The farther we buried ourselves into the thick, stormy night, the better I felt.

Instead of fading down, the storm that had accompanied us since we woke seemed to be picking up strength. We could hear thunder through the roaring wind, and we weren't sure how much further we'd be able to keep going. Lightning is a very rare event on Everest, but with climbing gear and metal oxygen tanks strapped to our bodies, it wasn't something to take lightly. As the rough weather drew nearer, we kept an ongoing discussion on our radios, eventually deciding to go just a little farther and see if it would fizzle out.

Despite our worries about the weather, I found myself continuing to feel better and stronger. The sensation in my chest was driving me on, and my pace started to pick up. Chris and Erik, who were immediately behind me, urged me to forge on ahead, so I let my legs go free and started passing some of my team members. Eventually I found myself at the front of the group and decided to venture out ahead a couple dozen yards.

I recognized a rock feature that would mark our halfway point to the summit. We had agreed we should stop there to assess whether we'd be able to continue. The thunderstorm we feared was still raging in the distance, but things seemed to be going very well otherwise. Despite the fact that we'd spent an extra day at Camp IV in the death zone, we were in a groove. Everyone was moving along at a brisk pace. I stopped to look ahead. Behind the electric flashes, a small dot of light was peeking through. As I waited for the rest of the group to arrive, it grew larger and brighter, until I could make out the outline of perhaps the most beautiful thing I've ever seen. The sun was rising just over the Everest summit, casting an inviting glow over the mountain. I spent a few awestricken minutes, taking it in before I turned to face my team. We all nodded to each other and, without a word, went on.

The feeling in my chest was like a small fire now, driving me farther ahead. My strides came quickly and easily, outpacing those of my teammates. Under the glow of the sun, I was free to wander farther ahead and remain roped in and within site. As I pushed higher, the storm that had threatened to engulf us had fallen just short. It was sitting a few dozen yards below our feet, spread out like a carpet under the ridge we were working up. The clouds were nearly perfectly flat, the lightning popping like squares on a disco floor. It was spectacular, but I wondered if my brain was suffering from oxygen deficiency. As a medical professional and someone who's seen 107 Grateful Dead shows, I know that not everything your mind conjures up under those conditions exists in the outside world. But, to my relief, my teammates were amazed at the same awesome sight. For those few minutes, we walked on the clouds.

All through the night, we'd been following a set of ropes left by a previous team who had chosen the same route. We didn't necessarily need them to find the way, but they would be critical for the descent if a storm were to move in and disorient us. At that altitude, a nice 80 mile-an-hour gust could push a climber directly off the side of the mountain and into a half-mile fall. Likewise, we could use them on the way back down from the summit. In whiteout conditions, a climber could lose his orientation and step right off the side of a cliff, as one had done the previous day.

I'd reached a point, however, where the ropes stopped. We were about a quarter of a mile from the south summit, a peak just a few hundred vertical feet and a couple of hours from the actual summit. The way forward was obvious, but the ropes were buried under a couple feet of snow. A new rope had been fixed, veering off onto a different path 40 feet to the left that led through a field of rocky shale.

I had come to what I call my leadership moment. It was my chance to choose the easy way, or to sacrifice for my team. I had been feeling great, and the short detour on the left would have given me a fairly quick trip up to the south summit, with the final summit just a short journey beyond. The sun had come out and burned away the clouds, leaving us with a clear, windless morning. This would be the best chance I could ever hope for to achieve every climber's dream, reaching the top of the highest mountain. But I knew from my years of guiding Erik that the detour route would be very difficult for him. The ground was almost completely loose shale. It would be like walking on broken dish plates, taking a few steps forward not only to get ahead, but to fight the tendency to slide backward. That kind of ground was exhausting for him, and I knew he might not be able to navigate it and still have the strength to push for the summit.

The way ahead would be great going for him, but it would mean digging out the ropes. In the thin mountain air, the effort would be excruciating. It would mean more than an hour of work, and I'd certainly be too exhausted to go on afterward. I finally understood what that feeling in my chest was, and what it was for. I took one more look to my left and the easy path. I followed it with my eyes up the south summit, through the small ridge beyond, and up to the goal that had been a dream for so many years. Then, I took a deep breath and let it go. It was time to dig.

I was surprised to find that I wasn't bothered by my decision. I'd come to Everest to help Erik get to the top, and my aspirations were secondary. I had done my job and would probably make it to the south summit. It wasn't the summit, but it was close, and I didn't need to take it any farther than that. I think it was in that moment I finally understood what leadership is all about. It's not defined by a title or a role, or how many people answer to you. It's about seeking opportunities to step up and showing your team you're willing to put their success above your own. These chances come every day, whether working on a mountain or in a cubicle, you just have to take them.

With the decision made, I started to chop into the ice and pull the ropes free. It was tedious and tiring, but also comforting to know my long trip was near an end. I knew with certainty I would not be able to continue on. My arms burned from the effort, and my lungs screamed as I drove my ice axe down again and again, freeing a few inches of rope with each blow Finally, I neared the end of the digging as the team caught up from behind. As the first climbers came within a few yards, I broke the last block of ice, springing the rope up in a taught line to the south summit. The work was finished, and so was I. I could barely breathe, and even the sensation in my chest that had given me such a deep well of strength was exhausted.

I fell down to my knees. I looked back to my climbing partners and a huge wave of satisfaction rolled over me. One by one, they came to me as they realized what had happened, and offered their thanks. Erik had been last on the line and was the final teammate to reach me.

He asked if I could go on, although he had to have known I was depleted. Looking across the ridge, I knew I couldn't make it. It was possible I'd reach the top, but I'd never have the strength to get back down.

Beneath my mask, I tried to force a smile. "Tagging the summit is optional," I answered, "but going home isn't." Neither of us spoke for a moment. After everything we'd gone through together, it was finally time to reach the highest point, and I'd given it up for him.

Erik looked back to me. "Can you get down?" he asked, the pain evident in his voice. I told him I could. He seemed to be trying to undo the moment, not wanting to accept the situation.

And then, my friend did the only thing he could: he thanked me, gave me a hug, and went to finish his ascent.

I sat on my knees watching Chris and Erik catch up with the rest of the group at the south summit. From there, it would be a two-hour climb across a daunting ridge, followed by a short climb to the top. I couldn't believe he was actually going to do it. After all the experts and critics had told us why it would be impossible, he was going to beat this thing. I was in no hurry to make my way down, just taking in the calm and quiet of the setting. The summit pyramid seemed so close I could touch it, sitting like a jewel with the moon hanging just above it. From so near the top, I could see the deep shadow it cast over Nepal, holding miles and miles in darkness hours after daybreak. I wondered if Everest would cast a shadow in my life as well, knowing I'd made it so close to the top without succeeding.

As I pondered this, the group reached the south summit. Erik turned back one last time to wave in my direction, and then continued on. I knew he was going to reach the top, and I wanted more than anything to share that moment with him.

At the risk of sounding mystical, I feel that life gives you a nudge sometimes. I've always tried to keep watch for those times when the world seems to be speaking to me, and this was one of them. After sitting in resignation for nearly 5 minutes, some of my strength had returned. I didn't know if it was enough for me to make it, but I didn't want to spend the rest of my life wondering. With my last bit of strength, I rose to meet and followed behind.

Beyond the south summit, the ridge you follow toward the top becomes very steep very quickly. One wrong step to the right wins you a 10,000-foot drop into Tibet, while the prize for slipping to the left is a 6,000-foot fall into Nepal. If I fell, I was convinced it was probably going to hurt pretty badly. I thought of this as I tried to settle my rubbery legs and make my way through.

It only took about an hour to catch up to the rest of the group. I fell in behind Erik and Chris. If there were any questions about why I'd changed my mind, my teammates kept them to themselves. We were all too exhausted to have the conversation.

Past the ridge lay the Hillary Step, the most famous 40 feet of climbing granite in the world. When Sir Edmund and his team first scaled the mountain in 1953, the Englishman relied on aerial reconnaissance to map out routes to the top. The photos available at the time had masked the short rock face that serves as the last barrier to the summit. With no way around it, he simply powered his way over it to reach the top. The face has borne his name ever since.

I had always thought if I reached the Step, I would climb it gracefully. I wanted to approach it like a work of art, a sort of climbing ballet. In reality, by the time I arrived, my body felt beat up and ruined. Unable to muster any technique or finesse, I embarked upon the ugliest piece of climbing you've ever seen. I flopped my arms upward, like a fish on the deck of a boat, hoping my hand would find some grip. Slowly and painfully, I heaved and convulsed my way up over the granite face in a grotesque exhibition. I think I even tried to use Erik's foot as a hold a couple of times. In the end it didn't matter, because 30 minutes later I was standing on top of the world with a blind man.

And you know what the first thing that guy said to me when we finally pulled on to the summit...

"Dang man. The view is just overrated."

We laughed till we had no more breath.

The summit of Mount Everest was unbelievable, but not for the reasons you'd think. It's not the being there that made it special, but the getting there. The place itself is a small flat area, no more than three feet by three feet. As you're walking up the last ridge you simply reach a point where you can't go any higher or farther—and you're at the highest point on Earth. Erik and I hugged, and we each shed a few tears that froze to our cheeks. We both knew we'd taken the long route to the top.

A lot of climbers say they go up big mountains to take in the spectacular views from top. I think these people are selling themselves short. Erik would be the first to tell you the view from any summit is overrated, and while I doubt his credentials for making that claim, I agree with him wholeheartedly. The view is incredible, but it isn't worth what we went through for almost three months to get there, and it certainly isn't worth risking your life in the death zone to see. The only thing that makes Everest, or any adventure worth it, is the chance to challenge yourself and take in the experience.

MountainVision

I'm often asked what I thought about on the summit. For the longest time, I tried to think of a profound answer to that question. I wanted to tell people that a life-changing secret was bestowed upon me by the climbing gods, or that I felt some deep wisdom fill me. Sadly, that's not the case. The reality is, after I'd taken a moment to celebrate and posed for a few photos, the only thought that came to me was, Now, how in the hell am I going to get down?

Erik, Eric, Luis, and Jeff on the summit of Everest.

You see, when you get to the summit, you're only halfway there. You've gotten all the way up the mountain, but you still have to get all the way down, which is often the hardest part. Three-quarters of all mountaineering accidents happen after the ascent. It isn't that the terrain is any tougher than before, it's because human nature sets in. People are exhausted and become complacent. They've already done what they came to do, so they lose focus and stop watching their feet. It's not unusual for a climber to make a major assault on a technically difficult summit and then walk off a cliff, get caught in a storm, or simply fall and slide off the side of a ridge. People think enlightenment comes to you at the top of a mountain, but it's actually the one place on a mountain where you don't learn very much.

Jeff Evans

Everest casts a long

Most of us are given a handful of summits in our lives, and usually we think of these "big days" as those that define us. Weddings, promotions, children's births and other completed adventures make easy landmarks by which we judge everything else. Nevertheless, it's important to remember that while we celebrate at the summit, the rest of life takes place on the side of the mountain. The challenge is to recognize that, and find a way to understand it and apply it to our lives. It's all those days moving up and down, all of the small challenges that make us who we are. Without them, the summit wouldn't mean anything. The real joy in your life can be found in the challenges, not the achievements.

PART II

EXPEDITION IMPOSSIBLE

At some point in all of our lives we receive an opportunity to attempt something this, all things considered, not particularly well advised. Some of us are wired to just jump first and see what happens. Others are far more hesitant and risk averse. Although some would consider me a guy who jumps at every chance to throw myself with reckless abandon at any harebrained objective, that is, in fact not the case. Especially as I get older. I carefully consider the downside to every task now and try to imagine what the return on investment will be.

That's why when, several years ago, Erik and I were contacted by a guy named Mark Burnett to do an adventure race based television series... I blurted out, "Um, hell no." Perhaps you've heard of Burnett. He's the television producer with many television series and movies to his credit with his feet firmly planted in the reality TV series genre. *Survivor* is his claim to fame. So I began imagining Erik and I bumbling through some race on national television, looking like fools in front of millions of people. The prospect of being on a reality show made me throw up a little bit in my mouth. There was no way I wanted to be a part of some *Survivor*-esque, voting-other-contestants-off, alliance-riddled game show. There just seemed to be no upside to the experience if that was the format, and I expressed this concern to Erik.

So initially Erik and I put Burnett on hold as we considered all of the downsides to agreeing to run across foreign terrain on national television. But then we realized that if we were to not agree to do this that we would be hypocrites to one of our main tenets... fear of failure should not hold you back. If we chose to not do this project, we would be succumbing to the fear of looking like fools. We would be allowing a perceived fear to influence how we operate. That's not who we are. That's not what we stand for.

Then we had a little Q&A with the casting director and learned that this show would actually harken back to the style of Burnett's *Eco- Challenge* race.

Now you've got my attention.

Erik and I have competed in several adventure races over the years, most notably Primal Quest, in 2004. After only sleeping 18 hours in nine days during *PQ*, I swore to never do another race like that again.

Clearly, I have remarkably short memory. We called Burnett up and told him we were in.

Once Erik and I committed to the race, we had to select a third teammate. We could have selected any number of our hundreds of very fit and capable adventuring pals, many of whom would have loved to be a part of such a big production adventure. We went with our new buddy Ike Isaacson, one of the wounded soldiers from our Soldiers to Summits project the previous fall. Ike had been injured in combat a few years back and seemed a totally capable teammate for this unique experience. The great pitch here was that Ike had suffered a partial hearing loss while in Afghanistan, so the perfect team name for us would have been "Deaf, Dumb, and Blind," and yes, I accept my role with pride.

The adventure was full of grand TV production clusters, some interesting, others ludicrous and pointless. However, the entire experience was exactly what we were looking for—an adventure.

MountainVision

The next several chapters are adapted from the journal I posted to my blog during the show.

CHAPTER 10

THE COMPETITION

The first episode of *Expedition Impossible* aired on Thursday, June 23, 2011, on ABC. The show was ranked number 1 among adults, 18 to 49, teens 12 to 17, and kids 2 to 11—the highest rating the network had on Thursday night since the finale of *Lost* in 2008.

The first of the ten stages in the competition was actually filmed over two days. The first day of racing wasn't too critical except the winning team got a five-minute head start the next morning. The teams that came in second, third, and fourth got a five-minute head start over the remaining teams. It's the second day of a stage that really matters because your performance on that day decides if you'll be staying or leaving on the helicopter.

As we rested in our Berber tent before the start on the first day, Erik left to go to the bathroom and Mark Burnett came in to have a one-on-one chat with me. Towards the end of our conversation Mark asked me, "Are you sure he's going to be able to handle this?" I said, "Yeah, I think so." Then Mark says, "Well I hope we haven't made a big mistake by having him here." Of course, I saw a great opportunity to fire Erik up by sharing this encounter with him, and I actually believe Mark made his remark on purpose, knowing Eric would hear about it. Not 100 percent sure, but if this was part of Mark's plan, it totally worked. When somebody says Erik can't do something, he tends to get fired up!

At this early stage of the competition, all the teams are checking each other out. We had seen each other in LA at the audition and again in a hotel on the way to Morocco, but nobody was allowed to talk to other team members. So Ike and I sized up the others for Erik. We laughed about the guys in knee-high purple socks, but, at the same time, they looked pretty fit. We also saw these giant guys, who we later discovered were NFL football players. We joked, "Big trees fall hard." When we happened to pass Akbar in the hotel, he actually growled at us, which was rather unsettling. It turned out he was totally kidding and is actually a super nice guy.

The first day involved the brutal sand dune climb in searing heat. Out of all 39 contestants, Erik was the only savvy one with enough insight to wear gaiters to keep sand out of his shoes. This may sound like a small thing but everyone else had sand piling down their feet, giving them huge blisters. Ike and I had to stop several times to pour sand out of our shoes. Blind dude gets experience points right out of the gate.

Did I mention how brutal the climb was? The show focused on Chad, from the Country Boys, suffering but I can tell you he wasn't the only one. Erik and I had just arrived from Colorado, which gave us a bit of an edge, but poor Ike was a flatlander and he really struggled. Of course Ike soldiered on—he's earned two Bronze Stars, a Purple Heart, and an Army Commendation Medal after all—but this raised the specter of a possible defeat for the first time.

The second day was really hard for Erik because it was super rocky as we descended into a valley. This type of terrain is difficult for him to move through quickly, and I got worked. At this point, we were about even with the Fishermen but eventually Erik couldn't keep up the pace, and they passed us. As they went by, one of them turned to us and with that thick Boston accent said, "Remember our names, we're the Fishermen. We're for real!" In my typical competitive spirit, that only made me want to crush those guys.

There were lots of early assessments on everyone's part. We can't fault the girl who wrote us off in the beginning. She said something like, "There's a blind guy on one of the teams, so I know we'll beat at least one team." Like a lot of people, she just had no idea what a blind person is capable of. As we got to know the Fishermen, we actually liked them a lot. They came across as Gloucester gruff at first, but were really awesome—sincere, hardworking, and the kinds of guys who you'd want around in a raging storm. They also had incredible fishing stories, going out to sea for weeks on end and having to be totally self-reliant. The Football Players were actually the nicest guys in the world. Akbar is a gentle giant, full of curiosity, except when it comes to all the insects around camp. All the creepy crawlies terrified him.

Our big mistake wasn't miscounting the snakes; it was moving too fast. We were among the front-runners, but this cost us half an hour. One of the things you learn from experience is that if you screw up, you deal with it. The reality was that three other teams counted wrong as well. However, the editors made it appear it was just us that miscounted. Guess I'll always be known for miscounting the snakes.

The faster you get over mistakes and come together as a team and figure how to remedy the situation and get back on track, the faster you're back in the game. I was really proud of Ike and Erik because we kept our heads together even though we made this blunder. Erik never blamed Ike or me for the miscount. He just took it in stride and powered on.

CHAPTER 11

LEAVING ERIK BEHIND

Yep, that's what happened. In Episode 2, I had Erik stay put while Ike and I took off to do the water challenge. The production team let us know this was a violation of the "20-foot rule," and we'd have to go again.

The fortuitous thing that happened though was that we happened to select the most water-tight bucket; so it still only took us one trip back and forth from the water source to complete the challenge. Every other team took two runs. So, it was a wash.

I know when I'm with Erik that my experience will be different. I have to check my own agenda at the door. I am on shift for him. I know that after 18 years of working with him, and I have accepted that role every day I'm with him. Yes, at times being with him requires double the effort. Sometimes I have to slow down quite a bit, which is tough for this competitive old boy to handle. However, adventuring with Erik has enhanced my experiences more than I could ever relate. When I'm with him my senses are heightened in ways that they never are when I'm not guiding him. I am acutely aware of everything around me, all of the things that could hurt him, or worse. As a result, the world takes on sharper detail. I feel threats; I sense danger; and I manage fear. I am grateful to him for enhancing my experience in ways that no one else can.

CHAPTER 12

IF HE'S WILLING TO PUSH IT, I'M WILLING TO TAKE HIM THERE

We were introduced to camels in Episode 1, however the creatures from Episode 3 were a whole different breed. I actually never rode a camel the first time around. I just walked in front, leading the train across the dunes. So as we arrived into the camel outpost, I was gearing up to take my first ride.

It was clear from the get-go that these camels were not excited to have anyone riding them. Erik's camel was trying to get rid of him in a similar fashion as the horse did with me in Episode 2. Erik got bucked left and right. We finally decided as a team that the safest and most efficient way to travel was going to be to walk these feisty creatures to our destination. Riding them was out of the question.

After Episode 3, Erik, Ike and I moved up to second place overall, once all of the camel riding, puzzle solving and dust storm forging was over. I remember this stage very vividly as it stood as the most freaked out I've ever seen my boy Erik, and I clearly have seen him in countless sketchy situations.

I was interviewed saying, "Erik is pushing himself exponentially harder than anyone else on this race. And if he's willing to push himself like that, then I'm willing to take him there." I've seen Erik go all out over the years, pushing himself beyond what I ever thought was possible. He has an extra gear that allows him to go further than what could possibly be anticipated. I've seen it many times. On more

MountainVision

than one occasion on this race I asked Erik if he could "give me a little bit more." Every single time he did. That dude has more will to push it than anyone I know. As much as he inspires folks around the world, he has inspired me countless times to take him further and higher.

Next week, the Atlas Mountains. I'm feeling good about our chances.

CHAPTER 13

IF YOU AIN'T FIRST, YOU'RE LAST

Well, clearly the past week has been full of texts, emails and calls from friends saying some version of, "If you guys don't win this mountain stage, I'm done watching." *Expedition Impossible* Episode 4 took us into the Atlas Mountains of Morocco, obviously the terrain that everyone expected us to dominate. We gave it everything we had, but second was as good as we could do behind those little Gypsie jackrabbits.

Erik, Ike and I knew we would be expected to do well on this stage. In fact, essentially every team approached me asking "Which way are you going to take up that mountain?" and "What layers are you gonna wear for the day?" Clearly, the other teams knew our experience in the mountains, and although it was a competition, I was happy to give them honest and sincere recommendations. Seeing folks succeed makes me happy. However, in the case of this race, I just wanted them to find success after we did.

A strange thing occurred in the course of this race; we got very close to each of the teams. The further we got into the competition, the more respect we developed for each other.

Especially our Gypsy Bros.

My favorite line of the episode is when Gypsy Eric tells me "Jeff, if you get a key on the first try, I'm gonna punch you in the face!" My response? "Well then, you better knock me out on that first punch."

MountainVision

The rest of that line, "cause I'm gonna come up swingin' for the fences" didn't make the final edit. At least a bit of the No Limits–Gypsies banter made it into the finished version.

It's clear that there was a lot of love between our two teams. We genuinely like these guys, and although we are in full-on competition with them throughout, there was a lot of help and nurturing along the way.

That being said, I'm very competitive, so I was fairly pissed with a second place finish on the mountain stage. You heard it from Erik as he's interviewed by Dave at the finish line, "We wanted first, but I guess we'll take second." We were wanting better.

The next episode was titled "A Blind Man's Nightmare." Hmmm, sounds tough.

CHAPTER 14

SHEDDING A TEAR FOR ALL TO SEE

When I agreed to do *Expedition Impossible* with Erik, I knew I was going to be exposing myself on national TV for better or for worse. I knew that the redneck that hides inside of me would surely make an appearance along the way, and it has. I also knew that my foul mouth would probably surface at some point as well, and it has.

What I didn't expect or count on was having a good solid cryfest in front of millions of people. But just to keep my pride in check, there it was: Erik, Ike, and me, all crying like a bunch of housewives watching *Oprah* together.

I dreaded having to watch Episode 5 when we returned from Morocco, but I knew that showing three tough, mountain climbing, salty guys unabashedly sobbing with the cameras rolling would make for TV gold. That being said, crying over fatigue, frustration or illness is for folks that haven't spent 20 years suffering in mountain ranges all over the world. Certainly not me. If I'm going to cry about anything, it will be over my son. When it comes to being a father, I am a helpless little puppy and capable of welling up at the slightest thought of my beloved Jace.

So, when we heard there was going to be a reward for the team that came first into the overnight camp, we all knew it was going to be some sort of contact with our families. That was enough of a catalyst for No Limits to push even harder. At the start line, I told Erik I was going to push him harder than I had up to that point, and in typical Erik style, he agreed with me completely and was game to charge hard. Little did we know that the day's terrain would be the absolute worst possible bit of course that could have been laid in front of us. Countless miles of rocky, bumbly riverbeds followed by a few more miles of rocky, bumbly riverbeds. I can get Erik across any stretch of ground on the planet, but when it comes to long sections of ankle-to-waist-high rocks, we just can't move that fast. It was what it was.

Now, why did we leave the fish fossil behind and not bring it with us to trade for the fish? Because the instructions did not clearly say to do so. I was taking each of those instructions very literally. Only good thing that came out of that whole screwup was my comment about "just grabbin' a fish and start runnin'," but that was the redneck in me. Classy.

The fact that our boys the Gypsies gifted us the reward was an absolutely huge move. At the halfway point in the expedition, we had already spent two weeks together suffering separately during the day and then rehashing it at camp every night. We were feeling close to several of the teams (although not all), but primarily we were developing a strong affinity for the young Gypsy dudes as we saw a bit of ourselves in them and knew that their hearts were in the right place with regards to this crazy adventure. They weren't reality TV mongers. They weren't whining or complaining. They were just out there having fun and getting it done. We liked their style. And by giving us the reward and the chance to talk to our families, it cemented our feelings about their character. As a result, we will always be fans of John Post, Erik Bach and Taylor Filasky. Good guys.

Another touching moment that deserves comment is my man Akbar throwing all sorts of high praise over to Erik regarding his athleticism. Ak has played football at the highest level with some of the most extraordinary athletes in the world, so for him to say that Erik is superior to all of them is just a remarkably inspiring thing to hear. Another class act, Akbar Gbaja-Biamila.

Jeff Evans

Sorry to see our friends the Firemen go home. If you could find "real American dude" in the dictionary, these are the guys that would fit the description. They have a true service mentality. They really care for people, illustrated by the help they provided the Cali girls in last week's episode. And beyond that, they are just straight up funny guys with a razor sharp, Yankee style of humor that had me belly laughing on many a Moroccan sunset. I will drink beers with them at their firehouse at some point in the future.

We were now halfway through this thing. Only eight teams remained. Next week, we would be paddling some serious rapids. The last paddle section was tame, somewhat boring. Next week was real, Class 4-hard, scary. The only time over the entire expedition that I was nervous was just prior to putting in.

CHAPTER 15

NOW THAT'S TRUST

Imagine the Episode 6 scenario:

You are blind. And I mean lights-out blind. Not visually impaired. Not, "I can see some shades of light, maybe a few shapes." No, you are dark-as-night blind.

You are told that it's time to jump off a cliff into some water below. Initially you are unclear as to how far the fall is. Maybe it's 10 feet, perhaps 20 at the most. No big deal. Kind of like a high dive at the pool. You've done that before. You can do this.

Then your buddy tells you to follow him to the edge of said cliff. You can hear the raging water below. It sounds like it's really far down there. Like REALLY far down. You can feel space all around you, below you. Your buddy scoots up to the edge of the rock to take a peek down and spurts out a "Well alrighty then, my goodness, it's like a 40-footer. But it's cool, it's cool."

"What?"

"It's no problem dude. You will do this. You will do this. Chances are good you're gonna live through this."

Any rational person would say, "You are absolutely out of your mind." I mean come on. I can't see where I'm going to land. I might flip over and land on my back or head. 40 feet is a LOOONG way down. A lot can go wrong in 40 feet. No way man.

Well I suppose Erik IS a bit irrational. He's also got balls of steel and trusts his bro unconditionally.

Jeff Evans

I have been guiding Erik on mountains and rock faces all over the world for close to 20 years. Together, we have navigated what many folks would consider some of the most challenging and deadly terrain on the planet, much of it requiring VERY precise communication, a profound level of trust, and a willingness to execute with everything we've got.

You skootch over to the edge. Stand up. Hold your buddy's hand and count it down, "3-2-1-LAUNCH!"

Commercial break.

Jeff and Erik about to finish the cliff jump in Morocco.

This was a great episode of *Expedition Impossible*—lots of drama, excitement and fun challenges. The production staff did a great job putting this all together (shout out to you, Shooter). You can imagine the complexity of putting together such a huge operation. Quite impressive.

After the jump, we moved on to a very cool zip line and straight into a very sneaky challenge where attention to detail was mandatory. Ike took this challenge on and as he headed off to retrieve the key, I hollered out to him a specific detail about our symbol. Turns out it was a critical piece of the puzzle. Ike nailed it, and we were off to the fourth-class rapids.

MountainVision

Going in to the rapids was the only time during the entire adventure that I was actually a bit nervous. The water safety guys had come to me prior to the put in and stressed very clearly that there were MANY opportunities for folks to get hurt on the upcoming stretch of water, and more specifically, Erik could get in big trouble here. I would need to be razor sharp. I wasn't worried about me being able to navigate the water. However, I was genuinely concerned about whether I would be able to get Erik through it cleanly. Well, our descent wasn't particularly pretty. Erik did take a few swims, but we made it down. And we passed a few teams along the way and came in third for the stage. Not bad for such a challenging stretch of racing.

As we came across the finish line, Erik's voice was still trembling with adrenaline. I had lost my voice from hollering out commands on the river for hours. Dave says that Erik is a real life action hero, and right on cue, I put out a "Yep, he's Superblind." Straight up.

Previews for the next episode show someone sustaining a significant ankle injury. The speculation is that it's broken. Ladies and gentlemen, meet my man Ike. He's a stud, and you are about to get to know him. It's getting real now.

CHAPTER 16

THIS IS LOYALTY

Episode 7 was a tough one to watch.

This was where we would see Ike go down. I remember the anxiety we all had for him as, in spite of his injury, we continued to put dozens of rugged miles behind us, potentially exacerbating a previous injury and having lifelong repercussions for Ike.

It started out simple enough. Run to the other side of the Kasbah and locate a symbol "hidden in plain view" somewhere in the chaotic yet beautiful city landscape. After about 10 minutes of looking around with the binoculars, I finally caught a glimpse of it on the side of an ancient looking stone structure. We are off to the trucks and down into the hustle and bustle of the city.

Arriving at the *souk* (Arabic for market), we hop out and begin to navigate through the sweet sounds and smells of an enchanting Moroccan flea market. This is the kind of place I would love to have spent a morning strolling around and perusing. Instead, we are at a half trot, trying hard not to bang into the Moroccans and their wares. This was one of the many times during the Expedition where I desperately wish we could have just called a "time-out." Let's all just put the race on hold for an hour and enjoy this magical place: see it, smell it, taste it. Although we had been charging through the dynamic northern African countryside for weeks at this point, we had not had much of an opportunity to really "feel" Moroccan culture from the inside and I know from many years of travel to faraway places that a flea market, a place of trade and barter, is exactly the kind of place where you can see how a culture truly engages with itself.

But alas, this is a competition, and we have to keep the pace at a high level if we expect to stay alive. So we weave and bob, cutting around piles of herbs and antique metal features trying to be as respectful as a bunch of Americans charging through a market can possibly be.

"Sorry. Excuse me. Whoops! *Shukran* (Arabic for thank you)!"

I have to say, it's not exactly easy to guide Erik through such chaos without occasionally bumping or stepping on something or someone. Throughout the market jog we were met with a variety of smiles, looks of curiosity, and a few Moroccan phrases which were clearly along the lines of, "Quit stepping on my shit!"

Check point cleared; one-way "airline" ticket secured; and we were back through it again and over to the waiting Explorers. Here is where the game changed, in a big way.

As I got in the backseat of the SUV, I saw Ike disappear from view as he was getting in the passenger side door. I thought nothing of it. Once we rolled out, I could see that Ike was grimacing and clearly in pain. We had been charging through countless miles of super rocky and bumbly terrain for weeks now, where an ankle or knee injury was a high possibility (as evidenced by Gypsy John's twister two episodes ago, as well as several others). But in the most unlikely of places, Ike rolls his ankle getting into the car. And it's the same ankle that he fractured while serving in Afghanistan a few years back. Well, this sucks. Ike's a tough guy, and he seemed to be in a lot of pain. Erik and I probed Ike with questions. I took a look with the eyes of an ER physician assistant, and it sure didn't look good. He seemed to have laxity in the joint with lots of swelling and tenderness throughout. Game changer.

The timing could have been worse, however, as the next challenge was to put me in an airplane saddled up to my good friend Rashid and spill out the door to the ground. Ike had about an hour to rest and be evaluated by the medical staff.

Time-out. One of my favorite lines of the show so far: "I'm skydiving in Morocco. Sick!!"

Back to Ike. Once I'm on the ground, I am informed by the medical staff (who are all aware of my Emergency Medicine experience), that his ankle stability is questionable and he will need to be pulled from the race to obtain an X-ray. I have recently discovered that Executive Producer Lisa Hennessy trumped the med staff decision and allowed Ike to make the call himself.

At this point, we all know what kind of man Ike is. He is a man that has structured his professional life around "doing it all for his team." This is the kind of guy that you want on your team. He will not let you down. He has served in combat zones that would make a brave man retreat into a hole. He has committed himself to always being there for the men and women around him. He surely wasn't going to let some ankle injury keep him from staying up with his boys. At one point I say, "You would have to literally cut Ike's leg off to stop this guy." Once Lisa gave him the go (thanks, Lisa!), there was no question we were gonna fire and see how it played out.

Miles of rocky terrain, cliff faces and one perplexing challenge later (another kasbah), we rolled into camp in second place. Amazing effort on Ike's part. Erik became the second most inspiring person on team No Limits that day. I was surrounded by two men that are as tough as they come. A true honor. Ike is the perfect embodiment of a soldier: brave, committed, and tough as nails. We are lucky to have men like him protecting our country.

We all stood nervously near the finish line waiting to see who would take the flight out that afternoon. I'm not gonna lie to you, I was so hoping to see my Country Boys round that corner. All three of these men are stand-up: strong, considerate southern gentlemen that I will call friends for the rest of my life. Good ol' boys that are a great example of considerate, mature, and genuine young men. I was very sad to see them go. That being said, there will be other Country Boys appearances in the world of MountainVision at some point in the future.

CHAPTER 17

NEVER GIVE UP

I guess we all hear this growing up: "Come on Son (or Daughter). Don't give up. Keep pushing."

I have used this phrase as a mantra MANY, MANY times during some of my more miserable and lengthy climbs over the years.

But never has that phrase ever been so meaningful or urgently delivered as during Episode 8.

The last episode had us in the hospital dealing with Ike's sprained ankle and receiving the news that they were going to require that he be placed in a cast for the rest of the race. I assumed this would be a death blow for our chances to continue as there would be no way we could keep up the established frenetic pace of the remaining six teams. But hey, we would at least go out proud and holding our heads high with the way we performed.

Then we got the gear list for the first day of the stage and on it was personal flotation devices, PFD's. This meant that we would encounter water at some point during the day, which translated to time OFF of Ike's ankle. Our host/pal Dave Salmoni took me aside and said "Listen, this stage will suit you. Don't give up. Trust me on this. Just hammer at it and you can stay alive." Good advice, Dave. We took it to heart.

After a very cool rappel down the ancient walls of a weathered Kasbah, we hobbled down to the shore of Lake Bin el Ouidane where we saw the inflatable rafts. I immediately realized that this would be our salvation. Water equals ankle rest.

By the way, two dudes (one of them blind) in a "duckie" does not add up to paddling in a straight line. Even though it looked like the Football Players were the only ones spinning in circles, in fact all of the two-person "duckies" were struggling to hold a straight line.

About an hour later, we arrived at the island and found the fixings to build a makeshift catamaran. I love Akbar's comment, "First, what IS a catamaran?" Seriously. I have done a lot of adventurous things in my day, but sailing is not one of them. And to really emphasize that point, all of the directions were written in sailing terms: "booms," "jibs," "masts," etc. Huh?

I studied the pictures, and Ike, Erik and I seemed to get it together pretty quickly.

Our maiden voyage was not pretty. Our sitting configuration was awkward and inefficient. And I distinctly remember Ike having a HUGE rip down the back of his shorts so that his ass cheek was right in my face. I suggested we make a strategy change. Erik moved to the left and paddled. Ike moved to the right and manned the sail. I moved to the back and used the paddle as a prop. This made all the difference in the world. We actually started sailing. Pretty cool. Another bonus, I didn't have to look at Ike's ass cheek anymore.

Approaching the next island, a couple miles away, we were neck and neck with the Cops, as the Gypsies uncharacteristically drifted off in the wrong direction. Rob, Danni and Jim from the Cops were straight-up gamers. Even though this was just an overnight camp we all wanted that win something fierce. They would not be denied.

Both teams hit the beach simultaneously and the race up the bank was on. Ike took off. Erik grabbed my pack and we ran. I looked to my left in time to see Rob trip and stumble sprinting up the hill, and suddenly the absurdity of this scene struck me and I started laughing hysterically in the midst of a heated race. We were all going for it with all we had, racing up a scrabbly hill to win a mere three-minute head start the next day. Now, in reality we all know it had nothing to do with that puny lead out the following morning. It was all about being a hard charging winner—putting everything out there in the spirit of competition. As we pulled in and Danni drew very close to Erik and me, I'm embarrassed to say I actually elbowed her right in the nose. Uncalled for, you dirty redneck! Sorry, Danni. She graciously accepted my apologies, understanding that in the heat of battle, shit goes down. Plus, she is a tough-as-nails Boston cop. That helps.

So there it was. We won a "stage," albeit an overnight camp stage. We were psyched. Blind dude, busted ankle with a cast on, and we come in first. Awesome!

Off camera. That night, we experienced a fairly significant storm with high winds around 70 miles per hour mph and violent lightning. It lasted for a solid hour, and there was actually talk of evacuating us off the island, which seemed a bit over the top. But just as quickly as it started, the storm passed. Many of the teams had not constructed their Berber tents in a bomb-proof fashion that afternoon, and the wind toppled them down like toothpicks, with our sweet Cali Girls being one of the homeless groups. We offered them some tent space, and they took us up on it. Was nice having someone other than stinky dudes in our tent for once. They are a class act those gals, each one of them. All destined for greatness.

The next day's stage proved to be a hard one to swallow as we watched the excitement from the previous day's win get washed away within 20 minutes of the starting line. Every team passed us with ease as we were limited to Ike's hobbled cast. Although we were not "giving up," we knew that we would be unable to keep up with the pace as we watched others fly by us. Erik and I tried to comfort Ike with the fact that later that day we would be drinking beers and showering our stinky bodies. Ike would have none of it. "We are not giving up," he kept saying, punctuating hours of silence. It left Erik and I the space to listen, feel, and taste the hills of Morocco like we had not experienced them up to that point. Everything slowed down for the first time. It was beautiful and bittersweet at the same time.

Hours later as we were rounding a corner towards what we knew would be close to the finish line, we walked right next to the lake. I remember Erik saying, "Hey, since we've lost, why don't we take a dip and just enjoy this last hour."

I replied, "Let's just round this corner and see if there is anyone at the challenge area." Sure enough, when we did, there were three pink figures in the far distance. Holy shit, are you kidding?! How could that be? They had to have been there for over an hour. Surely they will figure it out any minute and be on their way. Let's go have a look.

Once we arrived at the challenge point, we read over the instructions, and they just made sense to me—unlike the Moroccan rope lock, unlike counting the cobras. I just got this one. Give me a map and a compass and I am generally going to be OK.

Much to the chagrin of our recent tent mates, we rolled in and just nailed it. We ran up the hill and came in fifth for the day to send them home.

Wow!

It has been ridiculously exciting for Erik and me to watch the finish with our friends here in Boulder. We were there and knew full well what had happened, but I still felt the suspense, couldn't sit down. It was so tense.

We know the idea of Never Give Up is something that should exist in all of us. We know that you are never really out of it if you just give yourself a chance. Well, Episode 8 proved that to me in a way I won't forget.

NEVER GIVE UP!!!!

CHAPTER 18

AND THEN THERE WERE FOUR

As much as Erik, Ike and I wanted to provide an exciting finish for Episode 9, we didn't expect it to be quite the nail-biter that it became—an all-out sprint to the finish line against the Cops.

Episode 9 began the day after our dramatic finish to oust the Cali Girls at the conclusion of Episode 8. So our excitement and sense of disbelief in how it all went down left us a bit drained, I believe. That being said, we were still committed to give it our all in Episode 9 and finish like men.

Paddling for hours in fast, large rapids was a ton of fun for us, and a further chance to avoid having to run or hike on Ike's sprained ankle. We made up some time on the Footballers and found ourselves heading up the hill to the first challenge in third place behind the Gyps and the Fabulous Crew. At this point, it was clear to everyone on board that there was a split in the camp based on general disposition and approach towards the entire adventure experience. The Footballers and Fabulous Crew were cuddling up with each other, and then of course we were very tight with our Gypsy bros. This was the way it went down at the end of each day at camp, and how the "hook a brother up" moments were distributed.

We saw this clearly during the challenge that took place at the top of the hill with the word decoder. The Fab Crew straight up told the Footballers the answer (banks), and Taylor from the Gyps gave me a huge hint ("Where do you put your money?"). So even though we weren't into the "alliance" aspect of the game, it was taking place organically simply because we truly respected and enjoyed spending time with the Gyps, slightly less with Football and honestly, not at all with the Fabulous Crew. I did respect them for the job they were doing out on the course and actually mentioned this in my best Fab imitation on this episode. Some thought it was funny. Some not. I don't care either way.

Once we hit land, just as in Episode 8, No Limits was not willing to concede, however hobbled we were by Ike's ankle sprain. We knew it would take another colossal mistake from one of the other teams to keep us in it, and that our determination to charge hard at all costs was not reasonable to ask of Ike. We watched again as all the teams passed us, and we accepted our fate as best we could.

Then comes the caves and tunnels. Super fun and very India Jones-ish. While scrounging around in the cave in search of one of the last remaining pottery jars, I watched as Rob from the Cops scooped the appropriate pot and jetted past me on his way to seal up the last remaining spot for the Final Four.

It was what it was.

I continued my search, found the last pot and rallied my team out of the cave, across the water, and overland towards the finish and probable showers and beers that night.

As we were loping towards the finish line I caught a glimpse of the strangest thing: the Cops, coming back towards us. Unexplainable. They should have crossed the finish line by now. They had at least a 15-minute lead on us. Why would they be coming back the other way, away from the finish? Something strange was taking place, and I was going to gather my team and hightail it to the finish. See what happens.

As we picked up our pace, we noticed the Cops were right on our asses, running as hard as they could. This in turn made us fall into a full- on sprint—or as much as a blind dude and a guy with a cast on can possibly sprint. Ike was like Forest Gump, charging towards the line, bumbling along with his cast splitting into pieces as he ran.

MountainVision

Our finish in fourth that afternoon was one of the top five most exciting moments of my life. Pure joy and satisfaction expressed in a victory dance where I spiked my GPS onto the ground like a football player, much to the chagrin of the production staff, which lost a $400 piece of equipment in the process! It was intense, and I have received countless emails, messages, and tweets about how cool it was to watch a grown man do a celebration dance on national TV. My happiness was uncontrollable. We had done it again, pulled off the unlikeliest of all victories and were moving on to the Final Four.

Now we have come down to the final episode. An odyssey that began months ago has now come full circle. We will battle it out with the remaining three teams to see who take the grand prize.

This will be one for the ages. I can't wait to see what happens!!!!

CHAPTER 19

SECOND PLACE NEVER FELT SO GOOD

The night before the final stage of *Expedition Impossible* I remember still feeling a bit of a tingle from our come from behind victory on Episode 9. Racing to the finish to beat the Cops had both invigorated and inspired us, but clearly it sapped a lot of energy as we poured everything we had into surviving that near defeat.

Now it was time to push that aside and focus on the all-or-nothing stage that was right in front of us. It was time to put up or shut up. The four remaining teams were in it to win it, and there wasn't a slouch left in them. Even though we had cut Ike's pointless cast off, we knew that we would be beat in a footrace and had to hope we could overtake the other teams on water and perhaps the expected cerebral challenge.

Our Final Four Last Supper was a wonderful "calm before the storm" event that we all sincerely enjoyed. Both the honest fellowship and the ridiculously tasty Moroccan meal that was prepared for us were a welcome respite prior to the hurricane of competition that awaited us the following day. The best meal we had had in over a month left plenty of speechless moments as we slurped and gobbled the amazing, locally- prepared dishes.

The air the next morning was thick with tension, even between us and the Gypsies, as we prepared our gear and our heads for the big day ahead. Everyone was tense. Not many words were spoken. The production helicopter made at least a dozen passes over our camp, which just added to the surreal energy of the scene. With camp sitting on the edge of a fairly massive lake, it was no mystery that we would be hitting the water pretty quick at the start. Once we lined up with Dave to get our "Never Give Up" speech, we heard that one team would get the boot at some point during the day."

What?

I could sense the overall group heart rate go up by several beats a minute. If possible, it got even more tense. I'm quite sure I glanced over at Akbar as he clenched his jaw with the look of an NFL lineman, and you could almost hear him say, "I'm about to tear some shit up." Alright then, here we go.

We got the go from Dave and down the hill we bounded, team No Limits hobbling as best we could with a blind dude and a guy with a sprained ankle. Although we got in the boat dead last, we knew from spending the past month with them, our friends the Footballers were not going to perform well on the water.

Initially Ike took control of the oars of our Moroccan tin boat. However, after a few minutes of spinning and lack of smooth movement, I took over and started pounding the crappy little oars with all I had. Ike manned the back of the boat and provided micro adjustments and distance alerts as Erik sat behind me and made sure I drank a ton of water and consumed energy packets every 10 minutes or so.

As I was hammering the oars with a frenetic pace, I remember thinking, "This is the last day. I can dump everything I have into this. Save nothing." And I did exactly that. My teammates hollered words of encouragement over and over as we fought against the wind towards the next checkpoint on the far away river bank.

About an hour or so later we hit ground and started to move up the hill to the next check point. As I climbed out of the boat I realized my back was in full spasm from all the heavy rowing. For the first time in our month-long odyssey, I was leaning on Ike and Erik as they assisted me up the hill while I was bent over in pain. We were a pathetic sight, I'm sure. Ike limping on his ankle, Erik navigating blindly, and me, holding onto both of them as we struggled up the hill.

The only good thing to note here is the fact that the Footballers were not even in sight on the lake behind us. In fact, they were so far back we were convinced they had run into some sort of problem with their boat.

No time to think about them—we had to move.

Our next challenge was to sift through a massive pile of gravel with a shovel to locate two different geodes. Now, I have built enough snow caves and igloos with Erik over the years to know that he can't shovel worth a shit. My back was in full lockdown, and Ike couldn't be expected to do all the shoveling himself, so we needed to empower Erik to at least throw some gravel around while Ike and I rested. The editing made it look like Erik just spewed his shovelfuls in chaotic fashion and although this is essentially the truth, he did get the hang of it at one point and provided several dozen effective shovels. Best blind shoveler the world has ever seen.

We found our amethyst geodes and motored off to the horse corral to secure our undoubtedly scary, stubborn, and powerful Arabian stallions. It was here we were informed that once done with the horses at the next checkpoint, the last team to arrive would be eliminated and it would be down to three. With a healthy lead over the Footballers, I reminded my team that we had to stay cool here and not get injured. A runaway horse or another horse throw and we would lose our lead and be hopping in the red bird.

Ike led us out with his horse experience, too fast at some points for the two non-horse-riding dudes of the group. He is so comfortable on horses. We were in full gallop for much of the five miles we had to cover on horseback. I enjoyed very little of this section. Horses kind of freak me out. Riding them at full gallop across sketchy terrain is very intense, and I knew the whole race could be lost with one mistake. Fortunately, we pulled into the horse finish in third place and remained alive. The Footballers were out, and it was down to three now for all the marbles.

Our Footballer friends were extraordinary athletes all of them. There were several occasions we thought we could just "burn them out" by running at full speed for miles straight. No such luck. You don't play American football at the highest level by being a sissy. Even though these guys, Rob, Ricky, and Akbar, had essentially zero experience in the wilds of the world, they performed like champions. I am proud to have raced beside them.

At the restart, we had to sprint up a hill about three quarters of a mile to the Explorers and drive for 22 miles to the edge of Marrakech. This was awesome. We got to rest for about an hour in the truck (all but Ike as he drove the SUV quickly in line with Fab and Gypsies in front). Once we arrived at our parking point, there were nine camels ready for action. Awesome. Camels. Hate camels.

Erik and Jeff charging through the markets of Marrakech.

The 20-minute camel ride into the Djemaa el-Fnaa Square never made it to the final cut simply because there was no change in the order of the team standings. It was just a bunch of white folks bouncing on camels around the city streets of Marrakech. I was actually glad to see this segment didn't make the cut as I remember constantly groaning with each lope of the camel. It was uncomfortable as hell, and we were essentially at the mercy of the camels throughout the ride. Hanging on and waiting for it to end.

And then it was time to dismount the beasts and charge in to the chaos of the most famous market in all of northern Africa. After being in the mountains, rivers and dunes of Morocco for almost a month, entering into the frenetic craziness of the market was a bit overwhelming and we all became rabid.

No Limits fell behind as the Gyps led out with Fab close on their heels. We ran and we ran hard, ducking, bobbing, and weaving through the throngs of merchants and tourists, and trying to step on as few people as possible. At one point I could see up ahead that Ike had caught up to the other two teams. At first I thought this was a good thing. We are still in it. But my adventure racing experience told me that blindly following teams in front without being confident in your own directions was a recipe for failure. At one point during the chase I looked for confirmation from a security guard that we were on the right path. Although there was a lot lost in translation, he looked at my directions and clearly said in Arabic, "You don't want to go the way those other teams are going. You want to go this way," with a point of his finger. At that point I tried in vain to get Ike to come back sensing this was a turning point. Who better to know the area and where we needed to go than a security guard. Ike was obsessed and unwilling to let go of the teams in front of him, so we blazed ahead, following the teams in front unclear of our own directions. It all became clear a few minutes later when I approached Gypsy John and he confirmed that we had in fact not reached a previous checkpoint and were missing a critical map.

In retrospect, it's easy to question my actions as I sit comfortably in front of my computer and remember that crazy day. Ike was laser focused and I didn't process clearly enough the need to stop us from our blind chase and recalibrate. I know now that if we had gone back the way the security guard said, we would have found that map and been heading towards the last challenge potentially 15 minutes faster and most likely changed the final finishing order.

But in the heat of it all we kept firing. Once I got us back on track and had the map in my hand, I continued to ask directions as time ticked by, unaware of the position of the other teams. It finally occurred to me to ask the people that knew those streets better than anyone—the kids. Magically enough, a cute little girl in an orange shirt quickly identified the specific door-frame pattern and began leading us through the maze of streets, alleys and dead ends. It was all coming together and we were running hard to find our last challenge.

Through the designated door, onto the roof, and a look down on to the garden area below proved that the only team to have arrived was our Gypsy bros. No sign of Fab 3. We were in second and they weren't that far in front. I strained to look at what it was they were working on and I finally got a glimpse, a traditional Moroccan puzzle box. Haaa!

Just before departing for Morocco I had Googled "Moroccan puzzles" and guess what came up on YouTube? A video showing how to open the box. Ike and I watched it a few times, guessing that we would most likely be confronted with one at some point on the journey. Little did we know it would be the final challenge of the entire expedition.

The three of us blasted down the steps below and came up to the surface with our nice little puzzle box, ready to put our skills to work.

Since we weren't allowed to start opening the box until we surfaced back on the patio level, I watched with a sense of disappointment and pride as my young pals unlocked their box, retrieved the key inside, and began moving their ladder over to the other wall to win first place as the sun was setting.

Ike and I finally solved the puzzle right around the same time we heard the massive cheer go up on the other side of the wall from us. They had won it. The Gypsies had won the inaugural year of *Expedition Impossible*. I was so happy for them. They had dominated the adventure, winning every stage but one. They deserved to win.

Strong. Smart. Kind. Intuitive. I think they represent the spirit of this journey so well.

We crossed the line in proud fashion—happy for our friends and proud of our effort. Folks had counted us out from the beginning, and we surely had to deal with a fairly tough set of additional challenges that no other team had to even consider. We just kept charging, staying focused and determined. Supporting each other and believing that if we put good energy out there it would circle back and lift us up when things got dark.

The most amazing part of this experience was absolutely the wonderful feedback the three of us have received via Facebook, Twitter and email. Countless, and I mean thousands, of notes from folks about how our efforts on the show have inspired them to be better, stronger, and more excited to embrace challenge. Parents that have told us that they have been able to have very meaningful conversations with their children about surrounding themselves with friends that will never let them down. Those are powerful.

Be Strong. Work Together. And Never Give Up!!!!

The second place *Expedition Impossible* finish.

MountainVision

Jeff Evans

We hosted a Finale extravaganza with our Gypsy brothers here in Boulder to celebrate both teams making it to the finale. We could think of no other way to spend this exciting night than with 500 of our closest friends, family, and the Gypsies. Executive Producer Lisa Hennessy joined us. Multiple bands, lots of beer, food, silent auction items and six dudes telling all sorts of *EI* stories, most of them true. And the best part about all of this? ALL proceeds went to our Soldiers to Summits project and the Gypsies' nonprofit of choice, Feed the Children. We were fired up to funnel all of the finale energy into efforts that are bigger than us as individuals and perpetuate the goodness that we experienced in the adventure.

PART III

TALES FROM THE TRAILS

Clearly adventure is deeply rooted in my gene sequence....

The next several chapters include stories of expeditions, adventures, and projects I've experienced since *MountainVision: Lessons Beyond the Summit* was first published in 2007.

These tales have all been adapted from posts to my blog, *The World of MountainVision*, at mountain-vision.com.

Enjoy.

CHAPTER 20

SOLDIERS TO SUMMITS

In 2009, Erik and I helped create the Soldiers to the Summits program, now part of No Barriers Warriors, to guide military veterans and active duty personnel on mountain adventures. I have served as expedition leader and chief medical officer for its sentinel expeditions to Lobuche in Nepal; Cotopaxi, Ecuador; Mount Whitney, California; and Gannett Peak, Wyoming.

Sunrise on the summit of Mt. Whitney

I have tremendous respect and a sense of "debt repayment" for the service and sacrifices of our military veterans. The next collection of stories is from my blog, *The World of MountainVision*. We lead off with the story of our adventures climbing Cotopaxi down in Ecuador.

MountainVision

As I cruised around the Ecuadorian landscape last month I was constantly reminded of how new land is formed over and over as the earth oozes its molten hot magma (insert Dr. Evil accent here) from the subsurface cauldron below. Fresh black lava fields are visible across the relatively young islands of the Galapagos. Massive lava tubes and ridges make for scrambling fun around the interior's curtain of volcanoes. It is a Geology 101 classroom that illustrates how the earth redefines itself on a regular basis, sometimes violently, sometimes subtly.

It's been a couple weeks now since we wrapped up the second iteration of Soldiers to Summits. Our objective was, in part, to summit the photogenic 19,347 foot Ecuadorian volcano, Cotopaxi. However, as with most mountain climbing expeditions, this experience was far less about standing on top of the summit than it was about the beauty and struggle that happened prior to even stepping foot on the flanks of the mountain.

Looking at this expedition in the rear-view mirror now, I feel a bit like each of us, at some point on the expedition, took on the form of that newly spewed lava—occasionally blowing from the top of the cauldron in a dramatic and painful way—other times simmering and oozing slowly in a controlled and even-keeled way. The end result is new earth—a kind of new person laid over the former one.

How often in this life are we given the opportunity to redefine who we are, metaphorically shedding a layer of unwanted skin and embracing the new self that lies beneath? I would dare to guess that every one of us at some point in our lives has embraced the thought of starting fresh with a new chance and perhaps losing a few bad behaviors.

It's typically a painful process when that old skin is shed and that fresh, nerve-rich layer if left vulnerable and unprotected.

Jeff Evans

Sometimes the proverbial Band-Aid will provide protection and comfort for a limited time as the healing takes place but we all know it's only a patch and just hides what really needs to heal.

Soldiers to Summits was established with the idea of providing a venue for healing. We strive to provide a positive and nurturing atmosphere where individuals can peel back that layer of dead skin, expose their rawness, and allow a new layer of protection to grow and flourish. As the program continues to discover how to best serve our servicemen and women, it goes through the same type of building process as those who are served by the program. We don't have it totally right just yet, but reflecting back on our recent journey, I am proud to say I was able to create some new skin through this expedition. I also watched with great satisfaction and respect as several Band-Aids were pulled off of some our veterans—sometimes very painfully.

 Growth is not pain free. Making changes is not for sissies. I think the earth and its metamorphic process is a powerful example of how to handle it. I understand that with a build-up of pressure, there has to be an outlet. New lava has to flow. Sometimes a volcano will blow its top and shit will absolutely go down. Other times, slow moving magma will be how new layers are created. At whatever pace it happens, we are left to understand our new skin and how to use it to make the world a better place. The new terrain is ours to walk on. Perhaps at first we just might want to tread lightly.

Just wrapping up our second weekend of training with our new Soldiers to Summits crew and as expected, I walk away with a profound sense of admiration and a great deal of respect for this year's group of men and women. I can quickly tell that even more than with our inaugural 2010 group, this assortment of soldiers and marines has reminded me that although I am the guide—one of the supposed experts in our endeavor—I am truly the one that is learning and expanding through my participation in this project. Each of them has dealt with a tremendous amount of adversity and is attempting to stand back up in both the physical and emotional sense. As I have engaged with them throughout both of our training weekends I am reminded how resilience lives and breathes in these dynamic and thought-provoking individuals.

This round of training was primarily geared toward the physical and technical preparation that will be required to ascend our ultimate goal this December...the 18,000-foot volcano Cotopaxi, in Ecuador. Two full days were spent up in the cold at the base of St. Mary's Glacier (approximately 11,000 feet) both dialing in crampon and ice axe work as well as collectively scaling a nearby 13,800-foot peak. The cold and altitude were a constant reminder for the team that we are preparing for a mission that will require each of them to dig down deep to reach an objective that will be, at times, uncomfortable to say the least. And although none of them have any experience of climbing and high altitude, they each know that anything worth doing is going to require some suffering along the way.

One of our discussions on Day 2 revolved around adversity. This has always been one of the most compelling themes that I reference in all of my keynotes and teachings. I have learned much about how I personally deal with adversity in the 20 years that I've been guiding my blind buddy Erik on mountains, rock faces, and adventure races around the world. Together we have been kicked around on multiple occasions—consistently being required to find ways of dealing with serious ass whippings. Erik has always been a beacon of inspiration in how to use adversity as fuel—turning a clear, life-numbing event into a catalyst for success. I have learned much from him on how to be an "alchemist," turning challenging objectives into summits of success.

Our facilitator that day asked the group a hypothetical question as he was wrapping up the topic of adversity. He asked each member whether they would, if given the chance, ingest a pill that would guarantee a life void of adversity. Take the pill and you will never again feel pain or inconvenience. No more red lights, hairs in your pasta, or flat tires. No more cancer, trauma, or mortgage defaults.

At first, this seems like a no brainer. Who wouldn't want to walk through life never having to deal with the daily bullshit that we all encounter? You would be squeaky clean—on a permanent vacation. Easy Street.

Now clearly this exercise is to prompt the participant to explore the idea that adversity is a good thing. After some contemplative thinking and group discussion, most people would say, "No, I wouldn't take that pill. I need adversity in my life to make me strong." We would conclude that without some hardcore adversities along our paths we would become complacent and listless.

I'm confident that in his career, our facilitator had always received this same answer—until he ran into this group.

The first person to speak up against the usual answer was an amazing young man named Kevin. We all listened to him lay out exactly why he would choose to take the pill. He clearly and succinctly explained how he had experienced enough adversity in his short life and how, if given the chance, he would swallow that pill down in a second and apologize for being late. "I don't need any more adversity to get strong. I've been through enough, and I'm good with sailing on the rest of the way without pain and sorrow."

A few more folks spoke up in this same fashion and those that didn't say so in the big group setting volunteered the same response to me later in the weekend. It was unanimous amongst the group that the "No Adversity Pill" would be a big hit.

What I concluded that day was that in some cases, enough is enough. We can all agree that the adversities in our lives help to weave us into the characters we are. How we handle the daily grind challenges as well as the life changing, monumental throw-downs is what defines us as individuals. But perhaps there is a point where we have experienced plenty of hardships to provide us the fuel we need to combat complacency. I doubt there is a limit on what we can take—but perhaps there is a limit on what we need to endure to be great.

On our final night, we sat around a campfire and swapped some of our favorite quotes. All of them were meaningful and thought provoking, however one stood out to me, and I'm still blown away by its timeliness and relevance. John Masters is one of our 2012 Soldiers to Summits class. His quote from Teddy Roosevelt is the embodiment of our mission with S2S.

> *It is not the critic who counts; not the man who points out how the strong man stumbles, or where the doer of deeds could have done them better. The credit belongs to the man who is actually in the arena, whose face is marred by dust and sweat and blood; who strives valiantly; who errs, who comes up short again and again, because there is no effort without error and shortcoming; but who does actually strive to do the deeds; who knows great enthusiasms, the great devotions; who spends himself in a worthy cause; who at the best knows in the end the triumph of high achievement, and who at the worst, if he fails, at least fails while daring greatly, so that his place shall never be with those cold and timid souls who neither know victory nor defeat.*

I am fired up about our upcoming adventure to Ecuador with these outstanding men and women. And although I know we will encounter some adversity along the way, I'm confident this group will handle anything that comes their way like the true heroes that they are.

CHAPTER 21

HAITI

Who'd a thunk that riding waves with the "Godfather of Haitian Surfing", getting and fixing eight flat tires on our trucks, bailing our Haitian driver out of jail and being the second person to ever kiteboard the northwest coast would be relatively insignificant events on our Haitian Adventure Sustainability trip? These moments were but a blip on our magical and mystical eight-day journey.

Let me explain.

Prior to stepping foot on the island of Hispaniola, when I thought of Haiti, images surfaced of mystical ceremonies, zombies, voodoo dolls and for the past two years—devastation following the massive earthquake. After spending over a week exploring the northwest coast, I found all of these things and a myriad of other splendors that make Haiti one of the most challenging and exciting places I have ever been.

Other than the above, I really had very few expectations prior to arriving in Haiti. I had of course heard of the widespread poverty and the overall desperate situation that existed throughout much of the country. I had also heard whispers of the untouched coastline, specifically the northwest region that held potential for challenging and rugged activities—if you could get there.

The premise of the trip was to join up with some adventurous pals and tow along a wide assortment of adventure gear to explore and ultimately showcase the adventure sport potential in the country. If we could identify and ultimately showcase the wonders of the Haitian coastline, we would hopefully be able to confidently promote Haiti as a viable adventure-sports destination. Tourism is of course one of the most viable forms of economic infusion as it touches on multiple facets of a local economy—from the guy selling fruit on the side of the street, to the bar where we buy our beers, to the grocery store where we purchase our food.

Based on email conversations with several adventure minded Haitians and hours poring over Google Earth images, we concluded that we would bring mountain bikes, kiteboards, and surf gear in hopes of finding the right conditions and terrain to give each of these sports a go. By driving from Port-au-Prince around to the rugged western and northern coasts on very little traveled dirt roads, we hoped to locate the ideal destinations for each of the respective sports.

Upon arrival in the recently devastated capital city of Port-au-Prince, it quickly became apparent that even two years (almost to the day) of the massive and pulverizing earthquake, the city had a long way to go with recovery. Prior to the quake, Haiti was the poorest country in the Western Hemisphere with a history of corrupt government. The natural disaster in January 2010 was a setback on a massive scale and has left essentially no work and an economy in shambles.

All of this being said, there has been a lot of bandwidth put towards Haiti since the disaster, primarily in Port-au-Prince, in an attempt to provide basic necessities to its inhabitants. We were profoundly impressed with what Sam Bloch has going in the city with his organization Grassroots United. Not only do they provide a conduit for many of the NGO and relief organizations in Haiti, they also work to promote sustainability projects in the face of disaster. Building construction based on compressed plastic bottles, straw bale homes, rudimentary cement crushing machines and ingenious composting applications are but a few of the technologies observable on their organization's site. But in my mind, the most impressive sustainable project on the grounds was the aquaponics display. This self-contained system merges hydroponic food production and fish farming. Fifty- gallon containers are connected to a raised vegetable rock and soil bed through a system of simple hosing. The containers are filled with live Tilapia fish, which provide fertilizer (through their poop) for plants to grow in the beds while the vegetables filter the water for the fish. A tight, symbiotic relationship that demonstrates biomimicry in its truest form. It has some of the highest yields of any food production method and uses very little water with zero waste. Brilliant! Too bad this concept can't catch on everywhere.

Once we departed the "family" scene at Grassroots, we set out on our long, bumpy ride up the western coast towards our first multi-day destination of Môle-Saint-Nicolas on the northwest corner of the country. Within two hours of departure from our overnight camp at Gonaïves we stopped to repair a flat tire on one of our three trucks. Little did we know this would be the first of eight flat tires we would encounter throughout the eight days (you do the math), a relatively nominal number considering the rugged, bumpy-ass roads we were on for every mile of the drive.

After a couple of days in country I began to take notice of the similarities between the Haitian Creole and the Tanzanian version of Swahili dialects I have heard for 10 years on my trips there. I was told by our resident Haitian historian, Paul Clammer, that the version of Creole we hear in Haiti is a blend of French, the indigenous native language of the Taino people, and the Fon language of Western Africa, spoken by the slaves brought to Haiti in the 16th century. It manifests as a syrupy. blended language that is as foreign to me as Greek.

Paul joined us for the first half of the journey, as he wanted to explore the uncharted northwest coast in order to complete his Lonely Planet guide book on Haiti. You know a region has had very little activity if the Lonely Planet has yet to document it. We were fortunate to have him along as he provided invaluable insight into Haitian history, politics and culture. He detailed the mysterious form of religion we know as voodoo and how it often manifests with souls, spirits, sacrifices and werewolves (a.k.a. *loup-garou*). He also explained that Haitian national independence was more about the slaves seeking their personal independence rather than national sovereignty as was clearly manifested in the slave rebellion of 1791. It's like they said, "Listen Frenchy, having a nation to call our own is secondary to our own freedom. Back off and go away!"

And that's how it went down.

Towards the end of the second full day of being banged around in the cab of a pickup, I spontaneously became inspired to pull the mountain bikes out of the back of the trucks and do the remaining mileage into our beach destination of Boukan Guinguette. The GPS showed it was approximately six miles away down a dirt road—easy right?

Well—as is the case most times in the "world of wingin' it," six miles turned into a rainy descent close to 10 miles with a flat tire about six miles in. But when a flat occurs, what do you do? Play soccer with the locals. Three of us found ourselves in a heated game of "football" with the local kids in a field on the side of the road. They won. Beautiful.

Hours later we rolled into what appeared to be, even in the dark by the moonlight, a magical outpost on the side of the ocean. Our camp was already set up by our truck drivers so we could just step right into a meal of the fish catch of the day and a few tasty Prestige beers (a yummy Haitian lager). After a few beers we all made our way out into the water as a group under the moon and enjoyed countless laughs as it felt our adventure really began to come together in earnest.

The next day provided the ideal conditions to try our hands at the first kiteboarding jaunt in this part of the world, ever. Tyler is an absolute killer under his kite. He launched out and immediately proceeded to pop multiple launches of 20 feet or more while skimming across the water with great speed and style. Then it was my turn—not so much. I popped up and slid across the water for a couple laps just happy to get up and make it official. A few other team members got out and gave it a valiant effort but it all came down to

Tyler and his sick performance. The locals were beside themselves—never having seen a kite carry someone across and over the water in such a way. They laughed and screamed with excitement as they watched. Beautiful!

Side note—my GoPro camera which was attached to Tyler's kiteboard, fell off on one of his higher and more dramatic jumps on day 1 of our stay at Boukan Guinguette. I just assumed it was gone, gone in the depths of the clear seawater. We just received an email from the owner of the beachside restaurant where we lodged that the local fisherman found the GoPro on the ocean floor and returned it to him simply because they knew that it must belong to the crazy white guys flying under kites. This act alone tells you of the sincerity and honesty that exists among the Haitian people.

The next day was all about mountain biking complete with wicked single track (which I kept track of with my GPS), more flat tires and some cactus issues. Beautiful!

That night we had one final test prior to arrival into Port-de-Paix. A nighttime river crossing with the reputation for sweeping vehicles downriver. Well, alrighty then—This sounds like fun.

We watched with great interest as a few other trucks chose their lines and made the crossing—some cleaner than others. At its highest, the water seemed to engulf a small truck, easily flowing over the headlights. One by one, our drivers picked the zigzagging line that seemed best suited to them and went for it and each time the passengers filled with jubilation as they reached the far bank. Just another day in Haiti.

The next day we drove on more of the same (read: bumpy, dusty-ass roads), marking GPS waypoints along the road for potential single track rides as well as small villages where travelers could purchase food and drink. This type of mapping had yet to be done in this area of the country and I found it quite satisfying to be "adventure mapping" an area that had seen VERY little road traffic. All along the way, we were waving and engaging with local folks—many of them sporting very curious looks as three trucks filled with foreigners and mountain bikes putted along the roads and through their towns.

Our next outfitter of the journey was a young Haitian mountain biker named Tony. We were to depart the care of our wonderfully competent ground coordinator Cyril Pressoir and make the rest of the journey with Tony and his crew as we surfed and mountain biked around Cap-Haïtien. We knew things were about to get interesting when we immediately found that Tony's other driver was currently in jail for having an expired driver's license, and I would be placed in charge of the second truck's passage. Although I have driven in many countries around the globe, the road and traffic conditions in Haiti rivaled the most challenging for sure. I would have my hands full. But at least it was dark and raining. Sweet!

Two hours later—and after lots of Obi Wan Kenobi, Jedi channeling—we arrived, safe and sound at the lovely beachside hotel of Camiers Plage. Delicious ceviche, more local fish and a few more Prestiges and we racked out for the next day's venture. We'd be surfing with local legend Russell Behrmann, then a BBQ with an expat named Tim who has set up quite the utopia on the north coast.

After a mild morning rainstorm, we headed up the coast with Russell and a truck full of surfboards. To get to the spot, we had to descend down a steep, rugged, jungly dirt road to a small turnaround. As we were making the drive I commented that the ride back up was going to be a guaranteed "hooray," especially in wet conditions. Some foreshadowing to say the least.

Russell is known as the "Godfather of Haitian Surfing" due to his pioneering efforts at essentially all viable surf breaks around the country. It was a pleasure to see him move with ease from wave to wave as the rest of us fumbled our way on to a couple of the five-foot face waves. Surrounded by rugged coastline and dotted with remnants of 400-year-old French fortresses, it was quite the idyllic place to catch a wave.

As the late morning rainstorm came and went, the anticipation of an epic drive back up the road came to fruition.

Truck. Stuck.

MountainVision

The slippery mud turned into the consistency of Crisco and, as is common with Haitian trucks, our four-wheel drive feature had shit the bed. A couple of hours later and multiple tries with me behind the wheel (I was suddenly a pretty good Haitian driver) and the other pickup pulling my truck by a long strap, I jostled us up to high ground and we were safe. On to meet our soon-to-be friend Tim.

At the age of 22, Tim ventured over to Haiti in search of adventure that was seeded by a National Geographic story he had read a few years earlier. A few decades later, he has built what can only be described as a coastal nirvana. Tim has been resourceful and vigilant as he has constructed a "disembarking location" for the weekly Royal Caribbean cruise ships that visit the north coast of Haiti. Passengers who choose to get off the ship and "experience" Haiti are given the opportunity to visit Tim's creation of a "typical" Haitian village, experience his small but exciting "adventure park" (complete with alpine slide and zip-line), as well as visit the original landing point for Christopher Columbus as he bounced around the north coast of Haiti. Although some might perceive Tim's venture as contrived, I see it as an opportunity to employ dozens of Haitians as well as introduce an insulated American society to a more "digestible" version of Haitian culture rather than the poverty riddled scenes in Port-au-Prince (although I think it should be mandatory for Americans to the witness the latter as well).

We enjoyed our afternoon with Tim and his wife Kim very much—taking a ride on their 90-foot double-hulled boat and identifying another sweet location to kiteboard in the future. Unbeknownst to us, our new mountain biking guide, Tony, had been battling alcoholism for decades, and only in his late 30s, he and his family were suffering greatly from his disease. Right in front of our faces, Tony blacked out and fell down a set of concrete steps with his six-year-old daughter in tow. Miraculously, she was uninjured, and I found Tony to have sustained only minor abrasions and cuts to his face. This incident prompted an unsolicited but entirely appropriate and necessary intervention with Tony, facilitated by Kim in their living room, with all of us as witnesses. Although some may have perceived this event as uncomfortable and untimely, I, along with my group, found it to be an extraordinarily powerful and moving event. Kim was strong with her words. We chimed in when appropriate. Tony sobbed. I think—I hope—we were there to witness a life being saved that night.

It was around this time that Russell told us of an oft-used English phrase he uses with regards to Haiti, "comused." Haiti will confuse and amuse you, a perfect blend.

The next day we took two trucks loaded with mountain bikes up towards the Citadel (French: *Citadelle Laferrière*), the high mountain fortress built in the early 19th century by Henri Christophe to display the strength and sophistication of the new Haitian government. It's quite a sight to say the least. We guessed the mountain bike ride down the cobblestone road from the structure itself would be an exciting way to follow up a historical cruise through the Fort.

As our two trucks wound up the road the tropical rain fell and moistened up the circuitous, steep cobble as long drops appeared on both sides. All was going to plan until our truck rounded a corner and I immediately took note of about a dozen local Haitians running to peer over the bank at something.

Uh oh.

My gaze then caught the image of a white pickup truck just coming to rest on its side about 12 feet down an embankment in the thick of the jungle. My thoughts raced with images of Philip, Louise and Tyler stuck in the truck with unimaginable crush injuries. Not exactly the place to run a mass casualty incident and evacuation. I jumped out of the truck as my heart began to beat out of my chest, but when Philip stuck his head out of the upturned driver's window and calmly stated, "We are all alright." They each climbed out, seemingly whole and unscathed. The two Haitians in the bed of the truck had amazingly jumped when the slide started and avoided being crushed underneath. Miraculous.

What happened next was simply outstanding—and comusing. We watched as roughly 50 local Haitian men and boys connected a

MountainVision

strap to our one upright truck and began to physically push and pull the truck until, after a half dozen attempts, it was pulled back from certain carnage to being back up on the road and potentially drivable. At first look I said out loud that I thought there was no way possible their efforts would pull that truck out. Thirty minutes later, they proved me wrong.

Once the truck was back on the road another remarkable moment occurred. The workers, along with another 50 spectators, erupted in a joyous celebration filled with singing, screaming with hands raised in the air. It all appeared to be a manifestation of national pride and resourcefulness, essentially saying, "Look at us Haitians! We are small; we are poor; but we get it done!" It was quite a scene, one that I will never forget.

That day turned to night and we were thankful that another day of Haitian adventure had left us with vivid memories and no injuries.

I have been blessed to travel all over the world, seeking out adventure. And most times, I find it. In this case, it was on steroids. What a place, this remarkable country of Haiti. I am excited about its potential as an adventure sports destination. It is for the strong and rugged amongst us, not for the soft. If you want rugged and a taste of the unknown, I know the right place for you.

I will go back. You know why? Because I'm thoroughly comused.

CHAPTER 22

SUMMIT NIGHT

It's 1:30 in the morning and you're wide-awake. And it's not because you've been partying balls and have the munchies. In fact, you're lying in your sleeping bag, in a tent at 16,000 feet with a slight headache that just won't seem to go away no matter how many grams of Tylenol you ingest. The guy in the tent next to you is crushing logs so deeply you are convinced he is wrestling a Wookie, which makes your lingering insomnia even more frustrating.

On top of the tossing and turning in your stinky sleeping bag, you are racked with a cocktail of feelings and emotions.

Excitement, Fear, Uncertainty, Nervousness, Self-doubt.

All percolating in your sleepy head.

This is a typical scenario for most folks as they prepare for a summit attempt on a mountain with any substance to it. I have seen it play out for over 20 years including last week's Kilimanjaro expedition.

This was another good one.

As I typically do, I had planned out the staggered times of departure for our team based on observed pace over the previous week. Alpha team would depart at 3 a.m., and I would depart with Bravo team at 4 a.m. I downloaded expectations for the clients, established contingency plans for potential evacuations, arranged my African guide team in the order that seemed most effective, and so on. Dot all the i's; cross all the t's.

Then we step off—and it all changes. As usual.

Within 10 minutes from camp I noticed that one of my strongest returning vets from last year's Whitney expedition was dropping off the "peloton". I spent 30 minutes with him, trying to fire him up and coax him into lock stepping with me as I watched the rest of the 24 clients slowly pull away up the hill by the light of their headlamps. His legs just felt heavy and his motor wasn't firing. We've all been there. It just wasn't his day. We both knew it.

But this wasn't the guy I expected to drop off early.

Alas, strange things happen up high.

As I left my guy in the competent hands of my assistant African guide, I charged up the hill to join the rest of the team. And all was back to normal. The cacophony of folks pressure breathing. The shuffle of the dirt and rocks. The chant of Swahili song. All sounds that are so familiar to my ears on Kili summit nights.

And then ...

"Shit!!! Shit!!! It's out again!!!"

From 10 meters up above, I knew immediately whose voice it was and exactly what he was referring to.

It was Rick and he was reacting to the fact that his wife, Tina, had her shoulder dislocate. Again. This time at 17,500 feet.

A week before, in the midst of the pre-departure excitement of arriving at the gate and preparing to step off on this grand adventure, Tina had lowered herself down from the Land Cruiser using her left arm in a stressed angle and suddenly ...

Pop!

It was out. First time ever.

Now I've put a lot of shoulders and hips back in place over my 20-year medical career, but never on day one of an expedition at the entry gate, literally minutes before we were to step off on a seven-day expedition.

With about two to three minutes of manipulation, I was able to reduce the shoulder back in place. She showed her grit and strength during the procedure and once she was slinged up and her pack was handed off, she acted as if nothing had even happened.

The women are stronger. No doubt.

Back at 17,500 feet, the sun had just crested over the horizon, Venus was glowing red in the low sky and the coldest hours were behind us. The backdrop couldn't have been more magnificent—but the levity of the dislocated shoulder was significant.

We all breathed together. Calmed down as best we could. Situated our bodies to get good position on the shoulder and arm. And I got to work. There are several approaches and techniques for reducing shoulders and sometimes they are all needed to finally get it back in. This was one of those cases. I attempted the approach I was successful with seven days prior. Nope. No matter how hard I yanked on Tina's shoulder and how much pain I subjected her to—still out.

She went to a deep place. A deep meditative place that takes skill and experience to reach. A place that most of us won't know. I watched my wife go there during her 18 hours of natural childbirth. I've seen a handful of climbers go there during rescue operations off of Alaskan peaks back in the day when I was working SAR in the Range.

But a weaker person would have crumbled into a sloppy pile of blubbering shit. Tina did not. She stuck with me as I changed my approach. Again and again.

Thirty minutes went by and it was still out. I had run through my bag of tricks.

Forty-five minutes now and I was getting scared. Every minute that went by meant that the musculature and tissue around the shoulder joint were clamping down and making it progressively harder to reduce. If we would have been in the safe confines of an emergency department, we would have sedated Tina and administered some muscle relaxants to drop the head of the humerus back into its joint space.

But instead, we were leaned up against a rock in the dirt at sunrise close to the summit of one of the "Seven Summits".

In somewhat of a last ditch effort, I positioned Tina head to head with me, standing, facing me. I held her forearm with one of my hands and with the other I slowly continued to manipulate her shoulder. I closed my eyes. I prayed. And the Great Spirit, she listened.

Clunk.

It was back in.

Slowly I applied a sling and swath and started into the conversation with Rick and Tina about the next steps.

Clearly Tina was headed down. But what about Rick?

Rick is a tough dude. He is like me in the sense that his character is to summit. When he attempts something, it will get done. This is who he is. He was born to summit.

I offered to take Tina down and let him go up with the team and stand on top.

After a quick consult with Tina, he told me there was no question—he would accompany his wife down.

I was more than impressed with this decision. He chose commitment to his wife over his own aspirations. He chose to be a servant leader.

Badass.

OK, get them packaged up and set up with an African guide for the descent and get back to work with the team… who were now an hour above me on the mountain.

As the adrenaline of the shoulder incident ebbed from my body, I kicked it into a high gear and caught the team within 20 minutes.

And it was then that I realized I was smoked. My heart pounding out of my chest. My energy levels clearly effected. Not something I wanted my clients to take note of.

I shelved it as best I could and methodically walked the remaining steps to the summit of Africa.

The joy and satisfaction was palpable. Within our coalition we had a blind vet, a vet with one foot, several other injured vets, a 66-year-old woman who had never camped before and over another dozen other folks who represented straight up Americana.

I was proud.

Jeff Evans

But then came the descent. Oftentimes the hardest part. Physically and metaphorically. We must return home and share the story of the journey with those who weren't with us. This is not easy. How do you capture the feelings and emotions that are only gleaned from battle with yourself and the elements?

Summit night captures the spectrum of the human condition.

That's why we keep searching for it. We need to feel alive. And when the landscape changes in spite of our best efforts, we feel the most alive.

CHAPTER 23

IT'S NOT ABOUT THE MOUNTAIN

Typically, when a team arrives on top of a well-earned mountain summit, the moment is met with a loud chorus of yee-haws, high fives, and bear hugs. I've been a part of many of those scenes on summits all over the world over the past 20 years.

Not this time.

The 2014 Soldiers to Summits capstone expedition culminated last week with a summit of Mt. Whitney in California's Sierra Nevada Mountains. At 14,505 feet, it stands as the highest point in the contiguous United States. When I first accepted the role as the expedition leader for this year's capstone trip, I have to admit that I was a little uninspired with the choice of Whitney. Clearly it doesn't carry the allure or prestige of a Himalayan peak or the exotic nature of a mountain down in the Andes. However, our main sponsor, Wells Fargo, had requested in their support of the expedition that we keep our training and peak objective within the borders of the lower 48 states.

You bet. We can do that.

In preparation for our final expedition in the Sierras, the team came together for two separate training exercises in the Colorado Rockies. It quickly became very clear to me and my leadership team that this year's group of injured veterans was remarkable. We had selected well. Each of them embodied the characteristics that we strive to recruit for each of our S2S experiences: maturity, a willingness to grow and heal, as well as a solid, collaborative energy. More so than any of the past iterations of S2S, this team was ready to charge forward with solid intent.

We came together as a team during our trainings. We came together as a family while we were trekking towards Whitney.

The week we spent together deep in the Sierra backcountry gave us the opportunity to embrace the mountains and each other, learning, growing, and healing along the way. The mountains don't always give us what we want, but they always give us what we need.

As the morning of September 11th dawned, all twenty of us stepped on to the summit of Whitney just as the nautical twilight was starting to cast its glow over the horizon. We took those final steps and gazed east, watching the day dawn over a country that is still hurting from those devastating events of 13 years earlier. We paused to remember those that were lost both on that day and as a result of conflicts that sprang from the events of 9/11. In fact, the vast majority of the men and women on this trip had enlisted or were brought back in to active duty as a result of that horrific day, their lives changed forever.

I've been on bigger and bolder mountains. I've been on tougher and colder mountains. But I have never been as proud as I was that morning standing on top of that mountain with those men and women. Quietly. Solemnly.

We hugged each other, one by one. Very few words were spoken. There were many subtle smiles exchanged with a knowing glance. We knew why we were there. We were there to remember. To honor. To heal.

Because it's not about the mountain. It's about the people.

CHAPTER 24

SEEK THE FEAR, THEN POCKET IT

I've always looked a little kooky at snowboarders as a group.

"Yeah, that's cute—you in your baggy snow pants and flannel shirt scraping down the mountain and flattening out the bumps that us skiers worked so hard to carve out."

Snowboarding has always seemed like a little-brother sport to skiing in my eyes. That being said, many of my close friends were/are knuckle draggers. So is my wife of almost 12 years.

But the thought of me strapping into a board and sliding sideways down a mountain was as conceivable as me driving a pink Prius around the Blue Ridge Mountains of Virginia. Not happening.

Then, last weekend, my nine-year-old asked to take snowboarding lessons while in Steamboat. Then that same nine-year-old asked me if I was scared to learn how to snowboard.

Dude called me out.

Cool your jets, punk. It's on.

And before I knew it, I was strapped onto a board and sliding sideways down the bunny hill right beside him. Twenty-four hours later I was carving down a steep slope next to my wife with a big fat grin on my face, all the while trying to contain the fear that was trying to bubble over with each toe-side turn.

Turns out, going toe-side and heel-side (carving from front to back) are pretty sketchy maneuvers when you're not accustomed to doing so. I suppose it comes from the inert fear of slamming your fragile little noggin down on the hard packed snow at a high rate of speed. At first, each turn leaves you feeling exposed. But as with all things, it progressively gets easier. Every time you succeed at a turn you get more and more comfortable with it.

That is, until you catch an edge and before you can even let out a pathetic, high-pitched "Oh, shit," your ass and the back of your head slam into the snow simultaneously, causing a resounding shock through your entire body.

Then the fear sets in so that you don't go and do the same thing again.

Self-preservation.

Don't go and do the same thing that just catapulted you into the snow again.

What? Are you an idiot?

And thus I was reacquainted with my old friend fear or, as my amigos down south say, "*El miedo.*"

Fear is an evolutionary response to a threat.

Fear is designed to keep you alive. Epinephrine is injected into your body in large volumes when you're stressed or fearful. Too much of it is unhealthy. Extended exposure to epi or cortisol is bad for your kidneys, your skin, your hair, and your emotional happy factor.

However, small doses are good. That noteworthy metallic taste just as you commit to a scary action; it reminds you that you are in fact very much alive.

Yummy!!!

Scary shit has been happening to us as a species for hundreds of thousands of years. Historically, it may have revolved around being chased and eaten by a saber-toothed tiger or perhaps a few thousand generations later, it was running from a pillaging Norseman who was chasing you down with a bludgeoning hammer.

Nowadays, it's often less consequential.

Maybe it's the threat of your boss firing you from your unsatisfying but necessary job. Or perhaps it's receiving a $200 speeding ticket for going 55 in a 54 (thanks Jay Z).

MountainVision

Our moments of fear are cordoned off these days. We have to go seek out fear in our sterile society. We pursue activities like B.A.S.E. jumping, mountain climbing, dirt biking, and skydiving to get those primal moments of true fear, to get flooded with epinephrine and cortisol. Then we go home and relax on the couch with a beer in hand.

In my 20s and half of my 30s I sought out every opportunity I could find to get scared on rock faces and mountains all over the world. Fear was my friend. It was a drug and I was addicted. I used to love those idiots from the early 2000s with their "NO FEAR" stickers on the back of their jacked up F-150s. I would always think, "I'll show you fear, dumbass."

Then a wife comes along and it changes a slight shade.

Then a kid comes along and, whoa Nelly, shit gets put on lockdown for no other reason than "I don't want my kid to grow up without his daddy."

As we get older, the safety cocoon gets softer and "pillowier." It's easier to accept comfort and complacency. Why mess with comfort? Why risk my life? Why risk a broken bone? It takes five times as long to heal as it did when I was in my 20s. Even when it does, the arthritis will be a bitch. Not to mention, my aching back.

It's easy to let fear back you down. Our ancestors relied on that reaction to sustain our species. But now we live in a time when fear is sometimes consciously pursued, and once we find it, we have to suppress it. Ironic for sure.

I made a conscious decision when I turned 40 to fight complacency tooth and nail. Even though I knew I would never climb the same scary shit I did 15 years ago, it was up to me if I wanted to keep my instincts sharp and stay emotionally engaged with my environment. I would have to redefine the pursuits that would keep me challenged and excited. Part of that equation was to feel scared when doing an activity.

For me it came down to picking up a new sport every few years.

Five years ago it was kitesurfing.

Talk about fear.

After a half dozen hours of lessons, I decided to save money and just figure it out on my own in the dark depths of the Sea of Cortez in Mexico. I remember physically trembling those first few times out solo.

At first I was holding on tight. Scared of getting hucked around by the kite. Scared of getting dragged underwater. Scared of getting chomped on by a sea critter.

Then I let go. I quit holding on so tightly. I embraced the movement and pocketed the fear.

Once the fear was released, the joy filled its place.

Five years later, kitesurfing is my absolute favorite activity on the planet.

This year, it's snowboarding.

I noticed clearly this past weekend that when I held back due to fear, I would promptly be thrown forward or backward. Quickly. Painfully.

I realized after my first bumpy run (read crash-filled), that in order to make the turns, I had to let it rip. I found myself sitting at the top of the run saying out loud, "Don't hold back. Don't be afraid. Go hard into the turn. Commit to the heel-side turn." Once I embraced that, I was off. Carving. Cruising. Fast.

Not to say I didn't fall and bust my ass a few more times. But I felt the motion and I was hooked.

Clearly there are unhealthy versions of fear. The hours you lay awake in bed worrying about this thing or that. The things that you can't control. Those issues that seem monumental at 3:00 a.m. but are more manageable when you are up on your feet with a cup of coffee in your hand. Fear-based culture is disseminated 24 hours a day by mainstream media. Sociopolitical behavior is controlled by the fear mongers on CNN and Fox News. This is unhealthy fear.

Healthy fear is based on courage. And courage is not the absence of fear. Courage is doing that thing that scares you the most. Having courage to risk failure. Being courageous enough to fall down. Hard. And then get back up. Stretching yourself whenever you get the chance. Not necessarily with X Games sporting pursuits. It doesn't have to be kitesurfing and snowboarding. It's whatever you want it to be. But it has to scare you. Expose you. It has to contain doubt and a sense of the unknown. This is healthy fear.

Fear needs to be healthy. It's primal. It's one of the missing pieces of our primitive make-up.

See if you can remember the last time you were feeling absolute fear. That your life or limb was in perceived danger. For most of us, it's been awhile.

Go find that fear. Learn a new sport. Take a chance. Go toe-side. Get spooked a bit. Then pocket the fear.

CHAPTER 25

SHERPAS

Sherpas, the Nepalese mountain guides that make it possible for us to climb in the Himalayas, are often thought to have some unique physiological make-up or equipment that allows them to keep going at Himalayan altitudes.

They do indeed have something we don't, but it's not in their lungs or their blood cells. It's an attitude that pushes them to consistently overachieve. They treat every task as if it's the most important in the world, every person like they're a close friend, and every day like it could be their last. Sherpas don't do it for money and glory; they do it because it's a way of life. From the first to the last, they make it their mission to be worthy of being counted on. How much better would our world be if more people could adopt this attitude? In our world, it seems so important to take credit. Everybody wants to be in the spotlight, to get the biggest and the best. The real heroes aren't usually the ones getting the awards, they're the people getting it done every day. Forget trying to imitate actors and sports stars. If you want to stand out, be like a Sherpa.

Sherpas are a big part of climbing lore and legend. Ever since Westerners began flowing into the Himalayas in the 19th century to seek adventure, they have relied upon the local guides to help them navigate the treacherous terrain. While a few Sherpas have gained fame from their own work, most often they are the unsung heroes of the climbing world. They're always present and they always do the hardest work, yet they receive little of the credit.

My first experience with Sherpas came in 2001 when Erik and I set off to Everest. I was immediately struck by how much they seemed in contrast to their western climbing counterparts. Whereas American and European climbers tended to be loud and boisterous, the Sherpas were quiet and reserved. We would share puffed-up stories of our adventures around the world while they said very little, except to occasionally praise us for a well-told story.

While I realized right away that Sherpas had a very different way of looking at things, I didn't fully understand how helpful and wonderful they really were until I had finished the trip and arrived back home. I had just returned from Nepal and felt like I was still on the top of the world, literally and figuratively. I had gone to the world's biggest mountain, and with a blind man in tow! Wanting to stay in my rock star state of mind a while longer, I decided to take a look at some of the pictures our expedition photographer, Didrik Johnk, had sent over.

The photos told a great story. There were snapshots of the exotic places we'd seen, along with images from the climb itself. In one, we were crossing a deadly section of crevasses. In another, we clung to our ropes and axes while fighting our way up. And finally, there was a shot that captured us high on the mountain—striding through the Geneva Spur, deep on the mountain near Camp IV. I beamed with pride as I looked down at our photos, and was about to toss them aside when one caught my eye. Something seemed a bit out of place, but I couldn't put my finger on it. There we were, smiling wildly and being heroes. What could be wrong with that?

Then I noticed the detail that was getting to me. Standing in the background was one of our Sherpa colleagues. While we were whooping and celebrating under layers of high-tech, very expensive climbing gear, he was looking contentedly at the sky in a pair of blue jeans. And not even designer jeans, but a pair of knock-offs you'd find in a discount store. How could this be? I was bundled under several layers of Gore-Tex and goose down, all designed to keep me warm and alive in a place where life shouldn't be. This man looked like he was taking a stroll in the park. Mount Everest, especially near the top, is squarely in the death zone— complete with extreme cold, wind, and lack of oxygen. True, our Sherpa friend was carrying a canister of oxygen, but it was for me!

At that moment, I started to realize who the real rock stars were. Our Sherpa friends had shown up every day and done everything asked of them and more, without the slightest hint of impatience or complaint. My recollection of this is not unique. Every single climber I've talked to since, when asked, has vouched for the Sherpas' remarkable mindset. Their willingness to take on any challenge for the team without expecting recognition of any kind is an amazing trait. For them, nothing is ever too hard, too heavy, or too long.

Physiologically, many people think Sherpas hold a genetic advantage in the mountains. This idea was so compelling that a major study was done to examine them. A team of researchers ran many body composition comparisons between Sherpa and Western climbers, dissecting many of our basic human functions as they relate to high-altitude stress. After a solid year of computing and comparing, they found we are all basically the same. When I heard this, I couldn't help but laugh out loud. It just proved to me what I already knew: Sherpas have important qualities that are just not quantifiable. So how do they do it? It's simple; they outwork us.

CHAPTER 26

STARBUCKS

Heading home after a wonderful couple of days in the Great Northwest feeling stimulated and content from an engaging visit with the Starbucks team. Whenever I return from Washington or Oregon there seems to be this warm and compelling emotion that cool shit is going down up there—like a secret that the rest of us are just not let in on. It's rugged, hip and proud up there. My kind of place.

When one thinks of a truly global brand that is recognizable both in its logo, product and atmosphere—a brand that has succeeded in demanding a universal standardization for all of its employees to follow in order to achieve a destination for community and fellowship within its walls—Starbucks has to be in the forefront of any list. In my travels all over the world there is one thing for certain... when I encounter the ubiquitous Starbucks store (essentially guaranteed at some point in any journey), the soy chai ice coffee I order will taste just as delicious in Chengdu, China as it will in Boulder, Colorado. You know what you're getting both with the coffee as well as the warm coffee bean smell and soft music that fills the building.

It goes without saying that in order to pull this off there must be a solid quarterback making the calls for the team. I was aware of Starbucks CEO Howard Shultz and his creation and guidance of the global icon over the years. I was only slightly familiar with the fact that he gave up his role as CEO at the turn of the millennium, and coincidentally or not, Starbucks lost its unique character as well as a large portion of its share value. I had heard that he had returned to his role as master executive mid-decade and the ship had been recently righted. I really knew nothing more than this on the Starbucks saga and was quite oblivious to the mystique that surrounded its founder and leader.

Once I arrived in Seattle to provide a keynote to the Supply Chain team, I was alerted that Howard had requested a meeting with me in his office with a couple of his trusted leaders. I was honored and thrilled to meet such a legend of brand development but didn't really think much about it as I prepared my keynote and breakout sessions for the team. So I thought it somewhat comical when, the night before the meeting, my Starbucks host asked me, "Have you thought about what you are going to talk to Howard about tomorrow?" I chuckled a bit and said no, which prompted a very visible nervous twitch in my host's manner. After all, she was the one that set up the meeting. Her reputation could be affected by the success or failure of the one-on-one she had arranged between this unknown, dirtbag, redneck climber dude and one of the world's leading executives. A bit of a roll of the dice for sure.

The next morning as I strolled down the hall towards the CEO's office, I see this tall, gangly fellow in khakis and a casual, button down shirt walking towards us with a gracious and inviting smile. He looked happy and affable, but not exactly how I would draw up the master chef of a global entity that had $22 billion in sales last year.

"Hi there Jeff, I'm Howard."

And with that simple greeting, I immediately got it. This guy surely had more important tasks to tend to that morning but he had found time to carve out 30 minutes for me in his office, and had done the research to know my name and my bio. He wanted to get to know who this guy was that was coming to potentially influence his most important commodity, his team.

MountainVision

He was inquisitive, made a lot of eye contact, and focused on listening to me speak, even when I constantly tried to circle it back and inquire about him and his story. He wanted to know about my background, what drove me to climbing and adventuring around the globe. He was interested in my family; how old my son was. He wanted to know what components of leadership I felt were the most critical. He asked how my life experiences had crafted my message. He asked and he listened.

You could tell that Starbucks—its employees, and what the entire brand represents—is critical to him. He lives it.

I have been blessed over the years to meet and spend time with some truly transformational individuals who, upon meeting them, give the sense that they are paradigm shifting, world churning folks: Tom Brokaw, Dave Matthews, George W. Bush (disliked yes, transformational and charismatic, also yes), Colin Powell, Sir Edmund Hillary, Tom Robbins (my favorite author), George Bodenheimer (ESPN CEO) and Phakchok Rinpoche (second in line to the Dalai Lama) amongst others. Each of these individuals ooze charisma and clearly have that not-easily-quantifiable skill of leading and influencing the masses.

I have also met and spent time with countless executives that, although they carry the prestige and power of a big title and the paycheck that comes with it, don't incite enthusiasm and a willingness to go to battle from their team members. They wear their fine Italian suits and slicked back hair so as to look the part but seem to wield very little real influence except for that of fear.

After 30 minutes with Howard, I understood why the Starbucks team regards him as somewhat of a messiah. He lives for them. He asks them to join his family and represent his love child. He feels strongly that Starbucks represents diversity and community. He has a history of telling his shareholders that there are more important issues than the bottom line. He succinctly told a conservative, anti-gay-marriage stakeholder at a meeting, "Take your investment elsewhere if you don't value diversity and inclusion," as a testimony to the company's ethos driven home.

Jeff Evans

The time I spent with Howard that day wasn't really about content and discussing how either one of us facilitates or conducts ourselves when leading teams. I walked away from that encounter understanding the value that a revered leader places on human interaction and dialogue. So much of our interface these days takes place in the buffered and sterile digital world. We are losing the face-to-face encounters that define our relationships and build trust. I for one am making an effort to do more face to facing instead of type to typing.

As I was leaving the Starbucks headquarters I recognized one of Howard's assistants strolling my way trying to catch my attention. He handed me a copy of Howard's most recent book, *Onward: How Starbucks Fought for Its Life Without Losing Its Soul*. Inside the front cover was a sincere personal note from Howard that he clearly compiled based on our conversation. He was listening.

As I have poured over the book (which is the perfect balance with the other book I'm currently reading, Greg Allman's *My Cross to Bear*; these two guys have led very different lives by the way), I have already dog-eared and underlined multiple pages and paragraphs that are very synergistic with my style, message and life approach.

A few of the jewels from *Onward*:

> *There are moments in our lives when we summon the courage to make choices that go against reason, against common sense and the wise counsel of people we trust. But we lean forward nonetheless because, despite all risks and rational argument, we believe that the path we are choosing is the right and best thing to do. We refuse to be bystanders, even if we do not know exactly where our actions will lead.*

This is the kind of passionate conviction that sparks romances, wins battles, and drives people to pursue dreams others wouldn't dare. Belief in ourselves and in what is right catapults us over hurdles, and our lives unfold.

MountainVision

"Life is a sum of all your choices," wrote Albert Camus. Large or small, our actions forge our futures and hopefully inspire others along the way.

Dream more than others think practical. Expect more than others think possible. Care more than others think wise.

People want guidance, not rhetoric. They need to know what the plan of action is, and how it will be implemented. They want to be given responsibility to help solve the problem and authority to act on it.

In times of adversity and change, we really discover who we are and what we're made of.

That meeting inspired me to go on to deliver a very impassioned keynote to the Supply Chain team. Once the smoke settled from that event, I was given the opportunity to facilitate a breakout session for the SCO leadership team based on, you guessed it, servant leadership. Providing key characteristics of servant leadership to the team in order for them to enhance the way they interact with their various teams.

The day was a home run.

Leading teams is a unique and subjective process that can be achieved through countless styles and approaches. Some are effective. Some are not. Some influence partners and teammates through inspiration and buy-in. Others coerce subordinates through fear and manipulation.

I can tell you that my approach and style have been profoundly impacted by a brief, simple 30-minute meeting I had a few days ago with a guy who listens and deeply cares about the people around him.

That, and a really well brewed cappuccino.

CHAPTER 27

WILL THE REAL CIVILIZED CULTURE PLEASE STAND UP?

Just returning from a month of globetrotting to various remote corners of the world, mixing mostly work with a little bit of play. I'm grateful to all of the good people that I was fortunate enough to share time with scampering around some wonderfully inspiring alpine settings. I never tire of witnessing my clients and friends embracing the beauty and challenge of movement through mountainous terrain and interfacing with the hardy local folks.

This month was truly another wonderful collection of vivid memories and images of local villages and homes speckled on the flanks of mountains and hills on two different continents. The simple life that appears before us as we tramp through some of the more secluded regions seems so rudimentary to most of us with their lack of running water, cell phones, and grocery stores. It's easy to look across the valley at one of the thatch-roofed homes where sheep and goats are milling about and feel a bit of despondency for the inhabitants at how tough their life must be.

"It must be so hard to live in such a primitive way. Bless their hearts."

And then, if you're lucky, you have a face-to-face encounter with one of the locals. You see the wide smiles and note the sense of comfort in their eyes. You feel that they need very little to be happy. Food, shelter, and family. Undoubtedly, they experience pain and sorrow due to disease, crop failure and lack of health care, but they exude this sense of being satisfied with what they have in front of them.

On the second leg of my work month I was in Peru with a wonderful group of Gold Star women who are the living, breathing definition of resilience. Recounting the characteristics of these amazing women and their fortitude is another story entirely. One of these women has been sponsoring a Peruvian child for several years and decided she would try to meet the child and his family while visiting the Cusco region on our adventure. After many phone calls and much effort from her and the sponsor agency, the meeting was arranged. The rest of the group was invited to watch and listen in as the meeting took place. At one point during the meeting it was conveyed to our group that this was the first time this family had left their hillside village. The first time they had been transported by vehicle. The first time any of them had ever been inside a building or seen Americans (or white people for that matter). This beautiful family of five handled this "strange" encounter with dignity and calmness. I can't imagine how overwhelming it must have been to have a group of 12 Americans sitting across from them in a hotel lobby, smiling and asking questions about their lives. The children walked three miles each way to school every day, rain, snow, or sun. They lived modestly and trusted that the earth and Pachamama would provide all they needed to survive. These families value the opportunity to go to school and aren't afraid to work for it, while we complain if the bus is late to pick up our kids or our plane is delayed an hour. (Try walking from LA to Chicago the next time your plane is late.)

Unbeknownst to them, the world went on bustling and careening around them.

On this same Peruvian trip I was required to evacuate one of the participants from 13,500 feet due to a very significant medical event. After a fairly touch-and-go 24 hours, complete with early morning horseback rides and hospital visits, I finally tucked her into a hotel room in Cusco and retreated to my own room for some much needed rest. Not sure why, but I was inclined to turn on CNN just to see what was happening in the world.

Innocence is best served in the dark.

"Five hundred Palestinians are now confirmed dead in Gaza."

"Israeli soldier taken hostage and tortured."

"Fifty combatants killed while battling over an airstrip in Tripoli, Libya."

"Ukrainians place blame for downed commercial airliner squarely on Russia."

"Another commercial airplane disappears over Algiers."

"Female correspondent sexually assaulted by mob."

The news cycle played out. Then, as it began to repeat, I had had enough. It was all just vitriolic pain. Every word was contentious and coming from a place of anger and hate. Our "civilized" world was in complete disarray with no end in sight.

I reflected back to that sweet, wonderfully naïve Quechan family that would not even be able to relate to all the pain that their fellow humans were inflicting on each other. They were, at that moment, just lying down with the sunset, awaiting another day of planting, harvesting, and grazing. Nothing more.

As daily travesties against humanity take place, these families go about their business just as they have for thousands of years, oblivious to the pain, sorrow, and violence that is taking place around the world.

I'm not suggesting that western society should disavow our technology and cultural advancements and resort to a more underdeveloped way of life. Nor am I suggesting that I would trade my comfy life with my *campesino* friends. I would simply ask each of us, me included, to reflect on the simple nature of life and how we can become more civil with each other. Our needs are fundamental: food, water, shelter, and love. If we could live more simply and allow others to achieve their basic needs, the world be a much more "civilized" place.

CHAPTER 28

AVALANCHE OF LIFE

It's that time of year again.

My yard is full of glistening snow. A handful of my fellow Colorado drivers act like they've never driven on icy roads before. Flames in the fireplace are a nightly occurrence. And my backcountry skis are practically vibrating at me from my gear room.

It's time to hit the big hills, climb up them and then ski down them. And I'm not talking about shushing down slopes at Vail and Aspen dressed in your pastel unitard.

I'm talking about earning your turns.

Ski sweat equity.

Tele till you're smelly.

Skiing in the backcountry with friends is absolutely one of the most pleasurable activities that I pursue. Even when the conditions are less than ideal, i.e. bullet proof, windblown, or just cold as balls, it's still so much stinkin' fun to go out with good peeps, skin up the flanks of some big hill, and scoot down steep glades amongst the rocks and trees without the mayhem of an overcrowded ski area.

Other than the occasional gear malfunction or annoyingly painful foot blister, there is only one potentially ass-whippin' concern that is ever-present.

Avalanche.

It's a fact. Sliding down large faces of snow is very much fun.

Another fact. These same large faces of snow react to the laws of physics in a powerfully beautiful yet devastating way as they collapse and tumble on themselves.

I've been in two. That's two too many. I am making it my mission to never be in another.

This morning as I was reflecting on the potential for this season to be fat, and I'm talking fat as in fluffy, I started to consider the massive amounts of precipitation we have received here in Boulder County over the past several months, including the flooding that walloped my downstairs. The hope is that this trend will continue into the winter, providing us with blankets of fresh powder all season long.

I also dove into my annual avalanche data review, just to brush up on the nature of why and when a group of innocent snowflakes up and decide they are just tired of sitting where they are and take a fast ride down because all of their millions of snowflake buddies are doing the same thing.

It was then that I began to realize the interesting parallels between the nature of avalanches and the nuances of life. A few snowflakey pearls:

Understanding recent weather patterns
Months of history play into what is happening right in front of you. It's always easy to just look at things and people for what they are on the surface when in reality there are many issues that lead up to how things are manifesting right at this moment. There have been storms. There have been sunny blue-bird days with excessive heat. There have been days with high and swirling wind. Each day is its own event that creates the picture that we all bring to the table. Acknowledging the past provides us more understanding in dealing with the present.

Weak layers lead to fracturing
It's easy to forget that we all have layers upon layers of personality that surface from time to time. Although each layer sits in close

proximity to the others, they are all exquisitely unique from the others. In the case of a big ripper layer, it's always the hidden layer that is the catalyst for failure. As much as we try to hide our unstable layers, those are the ones that require the most attention. They are the ones that break.

Wind deposition can load a slope
Wind can deposit snow 10 times faster than actual snowfall from storms. Wind will drive snow into sheltered parts of the mountain in many different directions during a storm and deposit significantly more snow in otherwise unreachable terrain. Wind is sneaky. It picks up those sweet little innocent flakes and lays them down in a spot they didn't intend to be laid down in. It's the mystery variable that is unpredictable. Erratic behavior that leads to dangerous conditions. It's just part of it.

Being smart when traveling through sketchy terrain
Just because you're not on a slope doesn't mean all is safe. Many accidents occur to parties that are down in a drainage or runoff zone. It's the slope that's way up high and off your radar that can sabotage you. Being aware of surroundings and out-of-site terrain is critical. It's easy to become complacent in a "safe zone" and fail to recognize that the peripheral issues can slap you down if you neglect to stay vigilant.

Knowing when to stand down
Sometimes the pieces of the puzzle just say STOP. Go home. Many climbers and backcountry skiers have an internal voice that occasionally will beckon that it's just too risky today. Live for tomorrow. Ego and pride can take you up a steep slope and place you precisely in the sites of a machine gun of a slope that doesn't give a shit how badass you think you are or what mountains you've climbed in the past. Humility and recognition will place you back at your truck so you can plan for the next day out.

Being solid with rescue skills and traveling with capable teammates
I owe my life to the couple of guys I was roped up with in Alaska when I got tumbled down a hill towards a massive, bottomless crevasse. They knew how to self-arrest. They acted quickly in digging me out. They were reliable. Surrounding yourself with trustworthy and knowledgeable teammates is the only chance you have in the case that you are hit by a wall of snow. Also of importance here is for you to be reliable and strong for the other folks in your party. Careful with who you put on your rope team. A time will come when you will need them, and they will need you.

Risky but worth it. The ROI is high.
The funny thing about avalanche prediction is the more you know, the more you realize that avalanches are very hard to predict. You can only arm yourself with some fundamental knowledge and skills and be sure that the folks around you are also capable. Avalanches are like the funny adventure of life. They are unpredictable at best, but simply a part of the overall journey. Nothing worth doing is without consequence.

But in the end—it's worth the risk. Some of my very best days of every year are spent skiing down mountain slopes with my buds. Even though we all know the risk, the joy is deep and fulfilling. The risk is apparent. It's just a matter of acknowledging the contributing factors and embracing them.

CHAPTER 29

THE WATER THAT BINDS

Just before I boarded my flight back home from another successful climb up Kilimanjaro, I got a texted photo from my wife, Merry Beth, of our son Jace stomping around in what looked like a few inches of standing water in our driveway.

"Been raining for 3 days now. Our grass is loving it and so is Jace. Safe travels honey." Merry Beth had no idea the impact this deluge of water from the sky would have on our home and our state of Colorado. No one did.

My 14th Kilimanjaro expedition was just a pleasure as I guided up a wonderful group of women, most of whom were from New Jersey. They all performed well. In spite of my mild reservations about spending two weeks with a group of "Yankee gals," they blew me away with their kindness, humor, and fortitude. I was honored to stand on top of Africa with all 12 of them after a long hard summit night. I would return home with a smile on my face and sense of satisfaction assisting these good people in achieving a lifelong goal.

Then the real adventure began.

I awoke Thursday morning in Miami, where I was scheduled to deliver a keynote speech to a group of financial advisors the next day. My first night in a comfy bed in two weeks provided me the kind of early morning where I continuously kept rolling over and finding deep sleep, over and over again, that is until my phone rang and I saw that my wife was calling. Wait, it's 6 a.m. there, an unusually early hour for my morning-allergic wife.

"Honey, we've got two feet of water in our downstairs and it's rising fast."

"Not sure I heard you right. Did you say two feet of standing water inside our house?"

"Yes. And it's raining hard. And I'm scared."

Helplessness. That was my initial emotion. Then fear and concern. Then, it was time to problem solve and assure MB that we would figure this out.

Before I could even send out the help signal flare, my phone began blowing up with texts and calls from my friends that were headed over to help MB with the house. Friends who knew I was thousands of miles away and unable to take care of my family. The cavalry was on its way.

I heard multiple times from dozens of people.

"We've got this."

"What can I do to help?"

"Tell me what you need."

"I'm on the way over to your house."

As the morning unfolded I began receiving photos of a dozen of our friends hauling furniture to higher ground, crawling around in the muck to access soggy boxes filled with random keepsakes and artifacts, as well as making calls to our extended network to get the mitigation of the flooding underway quickly.

Throughout the day I continued to hear stories of neighbors installing sump pumps in my house to relieve the volume of water even though their own homes were still filling. Tales of friends taking 90 minutes to drive across town to our house in the middle of the night to deliver pumps and hoses, trying to find roads that weren't washed away. I received photo after photo of random shit from my hippy days being saved by the salvage team. I found it so poetically beautiful that many of my old "hippy friends" were finding my old hippy flotsam and jetsam saturated in the crawl space. They put their energy and love into ensuring that hundreds of old Grateful

MountainVision

Dead ticket stubs and photos from days gone past were given a chance to dry out and perhaps be saved. The true find of the day was perhaps the most beautifully absurd. My friend Avery comes upon a plastic bag containing a two-foot ponytail that, perhaps in an effort to never let go of the long haired hippy that I was in my 20s, I still kept in a box, deep in the crawl space. And now, I get to keep it for another 20 years, thanks to Avery.

I returned home the next night to a house in shambles and a wife that had been strong until she saw me and finally let out all of the tension, sobbing on my shoulder. She had been so strong the past 48 hours, not sleeping, vigilantly monitoring the house, and showing our eight-year-old son how to be strong in the face of adversity. I held her as the tension and stress of two days poured onto my neck from her eyes.

The smell of mold and mildew hit me first. Worse than any locker room you've ever stepped foot in.

My furniture and belongings piled all over the garage, pools of water surrounding stacks of soggy boxes. My dad's antique dresser dripping water from its drawers. All the furniture stacked high with the wood wilting with water. My son's children's books, lying soaked on the cement with all the pages stuck together. All of my medical school textbooks soaked from cover to cover.

Then it was time to step inside.

The living room was filled with mattresses, tables, photos, clothes, guitars, and gear. Not any available floor space left. The downstairs was a maze of fans, hoses, dehumidifiers, extension cords and soggy carpet. The water heater was ruined as well as the washer/dryer and HVAC unit. The toilet was off its flange in an attempt to allow the water to flow down the sewage hole. The tub was filled with a layer of brown muck.

Ugly.

Boulder County had been crushed by a flood of biblical proportions. "The 500 Year Flood" hit us. Over 200 folks were still missing. Countless homes were lost. Thousands of basements were flooded and property damaged. Colorado got beat up, bad. Clearly, it was going to take years to rebuild our roads and the communities and lives they lead up to.

But I saw something beautiful through the clouds. Something stronger than the power of a swollen river or a flooded home.

I witnessed love and compassion. I saw consideration and kindness. Well beyond my house and its efforts, the stories of heroism abounded throughout the Front Range. Daring helicopter rescues and life threatening rescue missions. Tales of taking folks in who had lost it all.

In the end, we replaced the drywall, carpet, appliances, furniture, and gear. These are just "things" that have only material value. We viewed all of the lost items as a mandated "spring cleaning" from the universe. Time to get rid of all the shit you don't need. A solid exercise for us all.

What I could never replace was the community that I saw rally in an effort to help out a friend. I was grateful and proud of our local folks. They were rock-star-heroes and I wanted to seek out opportunities to repay the favor every chance I could.

Then, we dried out and moved on.

CHAPTER 30

SOMETIMES THE WRONG ROUTE TURNS OUT TO BE THE RIGHT ROUTE

It's been awhile now since I came down from my 12th ascent of Kilimanjaro, literally and figuratively.

You'd think after a dozen trips up the same hill one might not have much original to report on. Well, the mountains remind me again that we are merely passengers on the kinetic train that is the alpine landscape, and we should never forget to listen to the lessons they provide.

This trip started like any other as my 17 new friends (clients) and I arrived without much ado into Arusha, Tanzania. I always love the excitement amongst the members of the group just prior to jumping into a new and challenging adventure. Over the course of a few meals, team meetings and gear checks, the anticipation builds until we are finally on the trail.

The first three days moving up the flanks of this magnificent volcano were smooth and easy, like the other side of the pillow. Everyone finding his or her groove and pace. I'm still amazed at how this mountain invites you to experience her moods and stages of emotion. One moment you are swaddled in a dense cloud layer down in the jungle and the next moment the clouds break and you are treated with a panoramic vista of deep valleys and rugged ridgelines. And then the summit shows its face, tempting, almost palpable, but yet, still a lifetime away.

I had built in a rest day on day three of our journey on the immense and beautiful Shira Plateau at around 12,000 feet. This would be a nice location for the crew to relax and give their bodies an extra day to acclimatize to the ever more challenging altitude. In the world of mountaineering, a "rest day" is actually a misnomer. Lying flat on your back during a scheduled rest day is counterproductive. The idea is to get up, walk, take photos, and get your blood flowing.

After a pleasant walk over to a smaller satellite camp, our expedition team was treated with one of the most meaningful events I have ever experienced in my years on the flanks of mountains. Two of our team members, Robin and George, had decided that they wished to express their commitment of love to each other by exchanging vows on Kilimanjaro while in the midst of their grand climbing adventure.

And guess who they asked to perform the service?

I have done a lot of things in my life, but acting as a stand-in preacher, now that was a new one. I was honored and humbled to be asked to be such a big part of this special event, so of course I said yes. Now I just had to figure out what to say.

I decided to stick with what I know: teamwork, allies, seeking out your bliss, and dealing with adversity.

It was a beautiful ceremony complete with champagne (non-alcoholic of course—better for acclimatization!), a personalized cake, and best of all, lots of singing and dancing with our African staff of 60. Everyone on the team participated and added their personalized wish to the new couple. They had actually been a couple for 13 years, but saw this as just the right moment to seal their love with a ceremony.

"By the powers vested in me, uh, by the majesty and brilliance of Mount Kilimanjaro, uh, I now pronounce you, etc."

The next couple days we slowly cruised up the mountain to higher elevations, getting in position for our ultimate summit push from Arrow Glacier Camp at around 16,000 feet.

MountainVision

Prior to embarking on this particular trip I explained to the newly minted clients that we would be attempting a route on Kili that is undoubtedly a bit harder on summit night than any of the "standard" routes. The Western Breach provides a more direct access to the crater rim at around 18,000 feet. By ascending this more direct route, one is required to do a few "scrambly" moves up several chest high rocks. I had done this route four times in the past and consistently got great feedback from clients as they descended the "normal route" that they were so glad we had chosen the steeper, more involved summit route.

The Breach had been closed down in recent years following a tragic rock fall incident that occurred down low on the route, and killed and injured several climbers. All reports were that this particular group was traveling in the most dangerous of areas in the heat of the day, which put them in a marginal situation. Years later it became clear that groups traveling through the fallout zone in the cold of the night would be "relatively" safe from rock fall. I decided it was time to start taking groups back up the Breach.

As we were getting settled into our high camp at around 16,000 feet, it was brought to my attention that there would be a German team ascending the Breach the same night we were.

What?

I should point out that only a couple dozen groups attempt the Breach every year since the rock fall incident. Of course, a group of Germans were headed up the same night we were. I so desperately wanted to holler out across the camps something about Normandy and kickin' ass, but I thought the better of it.

More in the role of the consummate guide, I headed over to chat with the team leader for the Germans, who happened to be Tanzanian. We discussed the need to keep a solid distance between us as the potential for rock fall was noteworthy and dangerous. He agreed to have his team leave at midnight and we would leave at 1 a.m. What I would realize 24 hours later was the Tanzanian guide's curious omission that they were actually attempting a much more technical variation of the Breach, one that would be made much safer with items such as crampons, harness, ropes, and helmets. Seems logical that it might have occurred to my new Tanzanian friend that we would actually not be close to each other due to our route variations and we could depart camp anytime either one of us wished. Well, that information wasn't shared, so I retreated back to my camp confident in the distances we would maintain throughout the night and therefore have a solid safety buffer.

One of the first things I noticed as my alarm went off around midnight was how ridiculously warm the ambient temperature was. Couldn't have been lower than 40° F. Crazy warm. Balmy, if you will. On summit night my mood always changes from jovial and perhaps even likable, to downright militant and sharp. Things get a lot more serious on any mountain for summit night. It's game on. I feel it and want my clients to know that chinstraps need to be buckled, and I expect focus.

Prior to our departure I had established teams within the team of 17. Groups of two and three would be cruising together on summit night to ensure a buddy system for both safety and the cheerleading effect. I then separated my staff of African guides within the small groups to provide some local support throughout the night. I placed my second-in-charge African guide, Dustin, out front. I have done at least 10 Kili expeditions with Dustin and trust him immensely with my people. He is solid for sure. I knew that he would set a good pace and provide front-of-the-line confidence for the folks as the night slogged on and folks got tired. I kept my head guide, Godlisten, towards the back with me as a floater should someone need additional assistance during the night.

I watched as the German team cruised by silently at 12:20 a.m. They build some pretty awesome fast cars, but as for punctuality, not so much.

An hour later, we headed out from camp with Dustin out front. The German's headlamps flickered well ahead on the upper flanks of the Breach. Dustin headed us up the same path that the headlamps had taken. Far left of my previous approaches to gain the Breach, but I thought nothing of it.

MountainVision

Two hours into it and all was going well. The air remained warm. The wind calm. My people had started out of camp a bit chatty and excited, and now the expected quiet had taken over as everyone realized around the same time that this was going to be a very long night and they should conserve their energy.

I began to notice a bit of a traffic jam forming up in our group of 23. It seemed as though the solid pace my group was maintaining had come to a stop to navigate over some harder terrain. As I got closer I saw that folks were justifiably slowing to gingerly traverse across a fairly tilted snowfield.

Well, this was interesting. I've never encountered snow on the Breach. Guess it's a variation in the trail to avoid that historically dangerous rock fallout zone.

As I got in position underneath the middle portion of my group to spot them as they made their traverse, I took a gander down the slope to see where we would end up should one of my pals take a slide right into me. We were looking at a 70-foot slide, minimum, down into a rubbled up choss pile. The resulting carnage would not have been a pretty sight. Not good. I was concerned.

Well, OK. Get that out of the way and we will be clear and free. I thought to myself how strange it was that the new route would direct folks through such a potentially dangerous section. At our next group dog pile, I assured my peeps that it would be OK and that we were done with all that mess. Hydrate. Nutrition. Back up at it.

An hour later, we reached an identical snow slope with a left to right traverse. Again. Same potential outcome.

We were off route and this was serious.

I huddled up with my African guide team and tried to figure out what was happening. They agreed with me that we were not on the conventional Western Breach Route.

Now that we are in agreement.

Dustin then admitted to me that he had been following the Germans up to that point. It appears they were taking a different route and now we were up in it. No shit.

I did think about turning around. Then I thought the wiser of it. Down climbing is significantly harder and more dangerous than ascending. Not an option. Up it is.

Over the course of the next four hours, my new friends charged hard like I've very rarely seen in the mountains. Most of these good folks had never experienced any terrain like this in their lives. They did not sign up for this terrain and yet here they were, being asked to traverse and scale sketchy, hard, 2,000-year-old ice with life threatening consequences.

Not one of them froze. None of them complained. They got their asses kicked and they kept forging on. I was so ridiculously proud of each of them.

I could finally breathe again once we arrived on the crater rim at 18,000 feet. No one had fallen. We had all arrived, albeit just a bit worn out. I had some tired folks on my hands but they were all alive and thrilled to be done with the most challenging section of earth any of them had ever encountered.

Another hour slog up a slope put us all on top of Uhuru Peak together, unified as a team. We hugged, laughed, and cried on that summit, all of us knowing we had just shared something remarkable. It was my 12th time to stand there on that 19,340-foot summit, but I have to say, it was the most remarkable. The pride and relief I felt were deep and fulfilling. I took in the images with my new friends and we began the 6,000-foot descent to our last camp.

We arrived to camp at around 4 p.m., 15 hours after we started, completely gassed, but over the moon excited about our experience.

That night at dinner, I owned what had happened. I explained in great detail how the night had gone down. I described exactly how each of them was put into such a challenging scenario. I told each of them how proud I was as the emotions surfaced up from me in front of the group. I felt a deep sense of appreciation for the character that was called from each of them. People stepped up in a way that neither they nor I could have probably ever imagined.

It is because of scenarios like this that I seek to take groups out into the mountains. We go on a journey together where the alpine world requires each of us to pull from something primal, perhaps go to a place that we have never been. This place is sometimes dark when you are in the middle of it, but more times than not it is replaced with light in the end. A realization that we as individuals can access physical and emotional strength from deep inside, from a place that perhaps we have never pulled from ever in our lives.

If you asked any of the folks that were on this trip if they would choose to do that same route again, I'm sure you'd receive a resounding, "Hell, no!" But I'm guessing if you followed up that question with "Would you have done it any differently?" I'm also confident each one of them would proudly say, "Hell no!"

I found out later that day that the German team had with them the necessary gear to do the route: crampons, harnesses, etc.

Ultimately, as a leader, this one is on me. A leader has to own his management team's decision making. My guys made some bad decisions that night, but ultimately it all falls on me. We are all fortunate it ended the way it did, with all of us finding our bliss.

Folks ask me from time to time, "Don't you get tired of doing that same mountain over and over again?"

No way. The journey is always different and the experience is always precious.

Sometimes the "wrong" route is just the route you were looking for all along.

CHAPTER 31

MAKING FRIENDS WITH MY NEMESIS

Sitting in my tent at 19,000 feet in the middle of the Andes Range in Argentina, I remember coming to the realization that the wind is my enemy. We were not friends, and we never would be. Seventy mile per hour constant winds were pummeling my tent with unbelievable and unrelenting force. This had been going on for two days now, and I was convinced that it had become personal. A gloves off, ass kickin', vindictive battle. And as much as I didn't want to admit it, I was going to lose.

This dislike of the wind was fostered early on.

As a child, I remember riding with my parents in my dad's T-top Camaro with the windows down on a summer day. My parents seemed to embrace the wind blowing around the car, enjoying the warm breeze. But I clearly remember worrying that the paper and objects in the car were going to blow away, maybe even me from the backseat. I didn't like the chaos that came with heavy wind. Around that time, I also remember being aware of the wrath of a southern, summertime thunderstorm. Immense lightening crashing all around, buckets of rain filling the woods and of course, my nemesis the wind, hammering the house with what felt like hurricane-force power.

I have never liked the wind and throughout my mountaineering career this animosity has been nurtured with countless events that have supported my contempt. I have had dozens if not hundreds of summits rejected due to high winds. I have returned to lower camps on mountains from up high only to find my tents and gear throttled beyond recognition from a recent windstorm. I have retrieved bodies from the glaciers of the Alaska Range that were cast down like rag dolls by the high winds.

No, the wind and I were not friends. And we would never be.

One of the things I have realized in my path towards middle age and the slight bit of wisdom that comes with my quickly populating gray hairs is that I refuse to foster negativity. I am realizing how important it is to surround myself with positivity, with clarity, and goodness. And I mean exclusively positive. By doing that, it becomes so very easy to push away objects or people that exude toxicity or anything of the Darth Vader ilk.

As I inventoried the good and the bad, I started on my culling process, jettisoning the bad and nurturing the good. Some were clearly defined on one side or the other, some were a bit harder to classify. Some required a change in my own perception; some just required getting closer to things and people that I felt held promise. Some required cutting the lines completely. It's been like a spring cleaning of the soul. I recommend just such an exercise. It's enlightening and cleansing to say the least.

Mountaineering and climbing were at the top of my list of "What brings me joy." As I reflected on my 20-year mountaineering career though, I realized that the wind was a variable that was the yang in my alpine yin. I knew that it was a vital force in the construction of the very mountains I was climbing and that through its forces, vital weather patterns were born. I knew that it had its place, and I appreciated its role in nature, but just not when I'm high on a mountain, please.

So I decided it was time to become friends with the wind. I thought on how to go about doing this. I had paraglided a bit a few years back and although that was flying and dancing with the wind, it was more about thermals and floating. There was way too much sitting around with paragliding. Too many other variables in play. I wanted to harness the wind. I wanted to seek out the wind and desire its presence. I wanted to hunt the wind instead of being hunted by it.

Then, I had a new thought as Merry Beth, Jace, and I were planning our inaugural trip down to Baja in 2010. We were heading to a small fishing village on the East Cape of Baja that sits on the Sea of Cortez. Los Barriles is known for fishing in the summer, but in the Mexican winter it becomes a hotbed for this crazy sport called kiteboarding or kitesurfing. This wasn't windsurfing with all of their cumbersome and unwieldy gear. This was a dude or dudette flying across the water, on a board under a huge, beautiful kite being powered by the wind and the wind alone.

Eureka!!!!

The more I studied kiteboarding, the more it turned me on. Within 24 hours of stepping foot in Baja I was in lessons. A week, and dozens of epic crashes, later I was finally getting up on my own and flying across the ocean.

Bliss.

It's years later, and I have now kited in Florida, Colorado, Texas, South Carolina, Haiti, and the Dominican Republic. I have not only made friends with the wind but we now have an intimate relationship. I seek her out. I look for her on websites. I jones for her when she goes away. I follow her to remote places.

I encourage everyone to do a soulful recalibration. Bring in the good. Dump the nasty. Embrace the things that scare you and don't be afraid to face the dragon. Joe Campbell would be proud.

Me and my new friend the wind will tell you. It's time to fly!

CHAPTER 32

SOMETIMES A 60-FOOT BARRIER IS STRONGER THAN WHAT'S INSIDE YOU

I felt the joy drain out of my body as soon as we rounded the wall and I laid eyes on it. Suddenly, reaching the summit with our 2015 No Barriers Warriors to Summits team seemed painfully out of reach.

Josh, Margaux, and I had departed the team's high camp earlier in the morning to scout the upper section of the route for our summit attempt the next day on Gannett Peak. The previous day had been spent eyeballing the upper crux of the route, a left slanting couloir that appeared from a thousand feet below to have an anemic amount of shitty ice protecting its access. Even from our camp perspective we were skeptical of the upper flank conditions. If that ramp of ice wasn't safe to climb, the summit would be unattainable.

Gannett Peak is about as remote of a worthy climbing objective as any in the lower 48 States. Our team of 10 veterans, five guides and two photojournalists spent the better part of five days trekking deep into the Wind River Range of Wyoming, passing through some of the most breathtaking alpine terrain I have ever laid eyes on. Every one of the 26 miles of the approach was well-earned, not the least of which was the final mile leading into our high camp. The boulder field was a linear mile of uninterrupted, VW Bug sized boulders that had the look of middle earth meets the album cover of *Houses of the Holy*. Our two amputees and one super-blind dude got their money's worth climbing up, over, and down each of the hundreds of massive rocks.

But in spite of all the fireball terrain and big-ass boulders, we arrived as a complete team into our high camp, tired but satisfied and excited about what lay ahead. All the lead-up work had been done. Training was complete. The long approach was behind us. Only thing left to do was power through a solid summit day and stand on top of our objective.

My concern for our route conditions grew deeper with each glance I stole of the upper route. As the sun cast down on the upper snowfield, the reflection off the snow mirrored a sheer face of what appeared to be very old, desiccated ice with a potentially broken up snow bridge leading to the climbable ice. The inexperienced eye would see it as shimmering beauty, beckoning for boots and traffic. But those of us with dozens of years climbing in various alpine conditions knew better. We knew that weeks of higher than average temperatures would have melted the seasonal snow away, leaving only the thousands-of-years-old ice exposed. This is the kind of ice that is hard, crumbly, and tough to protect. It's the kind of ice that only a few of the leadership team could handle with some minor effort. The thought of putting our 10 participants on this terrain made my hands sweat and my Spidey senses tingle.

Each of our hard charging participants have proven themselves competent and experienced in the theater of war, but their alpine climbing training consisted exclusively of the three training trips we had facilitated over the previous four months.

Not a lot.

Remember, our goal all along with No Barriers Warriors is not to make these men and women mountain climbers. Our mission is to provide them with a transformational experience that uses the mountains and rivers as a backdrop. Even from a half mile away, I knew it would be tough to get everyone up and down that section of mountain safely and efficiently.

It was clear that we had to go up and lay eyes and feet on the route. As the expedition leader, I knew that the ultimate go or no-go decision rested firmly on my shoulders, so I would need to go. So, on the morning of our rest day, Josh, Margaux, and I departed high camp to go explore the upper reaches of the mountain.

Fun, just straight up fun. The climbing was complete with low fifth class scrambling, glacial traverses, low angle snow climbing, and splitter blue-sky conditions. We had a blast over the course of a few hours gaining an upper position. We rounded the corner of the gooseneck headwall and finally got close and personal with the upper couloir.

Shit.

The first eye catcher was the 20-foot-deep, sunken bergschrund that separated the upper ice from the lower glacier. Bergschrunds are the features that form as the ice that is pasted to the steeper flanks of the mountain separate from the lower angle glaciers. Oftentimes there is a snow bridge that exists that provides easy access on to the upper slopes. The same snow bridge that existed when Charlie and Josh reconned the route two months before was still in place. But now it was a sad little one-foot thick, droopy, unsafe marshmallow.

Well OK, we can get over that. It will take some work to get everyone over and back across that thing, but we can do it.

Then we looked up.

Above the gap, we could now clearly see the condition of the ice that protected the summit ridge. Just as I had guessed, stretching from side to side of the couloir was 60 feet of glistening, boilerplate hard, 10,000-year-old ice. Dripping water cascaded down its face. Once again I thought of a handful of ways we could get our crew up that section of ice but I continued to stalemate on how we would safely get everyone down this terrain.

But dammit, we knew that if we could just get by that 60 feet of terrain, we would have a fairly cruiser ridgeline all the way up to the summit.

Might as well have been made of two-foot-thick glass.

Jeff Evans

I sat deflated as I contemplated the alternatives. Each one ended in the same observation, "We might be able to get 'em up that way, but there is no way to get them down that same section safely."

In typical Josh fashion, the 27-year-old former SEAL continued to suggest multiple alternatives. The best of these was climbing around the ice. "Maybe we can circumvent the entire headwall. Let's go check it out." An hour later and some fun rock-block scrambling led us to the edge of the headwall, and a 1,000-foot sheer cliff.

No go. Down we went, occasionally blasting out a "Fuck!!!!!" with disappointment. We had worked so hard to get here as a team and we would be going home without a summit.

Back through the sweet terrain and into camp to join up with the rest of the team, ultimately to tell them that their much desired summit, the same summit that they had worked for and dreamed about, would remain out of reach.

I wasn't bummed for my own summit aspirations. Over my 20-plus year climbing career, I have been turned around countless times due to unsafe conditions. I was accustomed to dealing with the "no summit blues." All the standard clichés were part of my long-developed alpine mentation:

"The summit is optional but coming home is not."

"The mountains make the music. We simply listen."

"It's about the journey, not the summit."

And yes, all of this is true, but when I broke the news that we wouldn't be able to summit, there was no cute little quote that would quell the disappointment the group clearly felt. As much as we had tried to frame up the possibility of not touching the summit, this was still a massive body blow to the group. Tears, frustration, disappointment. We all felt it. For many, it was just another one of the many obstacles that was keeping them from completing the ever-elusive "summit."

Then the magic happened. The team requested a participant-only meeting; all the leaders were asked to step away.

Thirty minutes later we rejoined the team and listened to them request an opportunity to venture up as a complete team to the high

MountainVision

point; to go as high as they could; to lay eyes on this piece of unsafe terrain; to feel the power of the mountain and let it judge them for who they are; to conclude that they had done nothing wrong in this journey; and to confirm that they had done everything right. It was just the mountain dishing up a shitty 60 feet of ice protected by a big-ass moat.

Then I knew we had done our work. We had set the table appropriately. We had invited our guests, and they had joined us for a lengthy feast. The appetizer was good: it whet our appetites and made us hungry for bigger things. The main course was delicious; we took in all of the miles and smiles and felt full. But alas there would be no dessert—the cake would not be served. We wanted to end on a sweet note but would instead have to reflect on the fact that our bellies and souls were full. We had feasted.

The next day I began what would be a two-day evacuation of one our participants who was sick as a dog and spiraling towards full kidney failure. He warriored through all 26 miles back to the trailhead on one foot, one prosthetic, a horse, and a shit ton of grit and will.

That same day, September 11th, the rest of the team climbed up to the high point, took a look at the bergschrund and 60 feet of ice, and said, "Yep, I get it. Don't want any part of that." Although everyone was still disappointed, the team had now faced that barrier, looked it square in the eye and said, "F You!!!"

I heard stories of how each of the team yelled out names of their friends, fellow warriors and family who had been lost or deeply affected by the events of that day 14 years ago. Powerful to say the least.

My best bro and longtime adventure partner Erik was the founding father of No Barriers. From the beginning, the tagline has always been, "What's Within You Is Stronger Than What's in Your Way." I know that's true most of the time.

But sometimes 60 feet of shitty, unsafe ice IS in your way. And it IS stronger than you. And it IS blocking you from reaching your desired summit. And it IS NOT moving.

Jeff Evans

This is a fact of life.

When we encounter these immovable objects, it's critical to be resourceful, look for work-arounds and think outside the box. Then, once we have exhausted all alternatives we have to come to grips with it. It's not that I'm OK with it. I just have to acknowledge its existence. It's not going anywhere. But we are. Moving on. Setting our sights on the next summit, the next objective.

And so we climb on.

PART IV

EVEREST AIR

As with most worthy projects, this one began rather innocuously. It started with a text from a friend asking if I'd be willing to consult for a production team that was hoping to film the helicopter rescue operation on Mount Everest for the upcoming season. *Well, that sounds like fun.*
It seemed like a low-impact, fun way to make a few bucks and perhaps even get to go back to my beloved Nepal.
 I'm in.
 I met with the production team and was provided the framework for their project: film a group of badass helicopter pilots and equivalently badass climbing Sherpas rescuing climbers-in-need from the flanks of Mount Everest. All this would be documented for a potential TV series on the Travel Channel.
 At first glance, it appeared to have all ingredients for a great adventure: a solid cause, an experienced team of professionals, and a big fat budget. As I continued to mull over the concept, I got hung up on the fact that these pilots would be transporting very sick patients without the assistance of a medic on board. This would be

akin to an ambulance driver picking up a patient, throwing them in the back of the rig, closing the door, and driving away.

They needed a medic—a medic well-versed in high altitude pathology—a medic that knew Mount Everest and the surrounding peaks—a medic that had a strong affinity for Nepal and the Sherpa culture.

Wait...I know a guy.

So I signed up.

I spent all of April and May, 2016, in Nepal working with this amazing team. The fact that the series aired on The Travel Channel was insignificant. I could care less.

We ran 38 rescue operations. Out of that total, we guess that we saved close to two-dozen lives.

It was fun, scary, intense, gratifying and worthwhile.

The following chapters document a few of the more memorable events from my two months in Nepal.

CHAPTER 33

I WORK WITH SOME VERY BAD DUDES...

To date, this was the most high-profile rescue of the season and showcased to the world exactly what I've known for months: our Sherpa rescue team is the most badass, highly-trained, hard-charging collection of alpine rescuers the Himalaya has ever seen.

Yesterday, we received a report that two Slovakian climbers had been hit by an avalanche at around 23,000 feet while climbing the extremely difficult southwest face of Everest. They were stuck; one was injured; and they were requesting a rescue. Based on sat phone reports from the climbers, they were perched some 2,000 feet above the valley floor, holed up on a ledge known as Bonnington's Plateau. They could neither ascend nor descend. A long-line helicopter rescue was out of the question based on the steepness of the slope and surrounding rock and ice. In order to rescue these guys, a team would have to climb up the technical face, secure the Slovaks, and descend with them to standard Everest Camp 2.

The five men on our Sherpa team have essentially been training their entire careers for this operation and knew this was the type of mission meant for them on Everest this season. Once they heard about the problem and what it would require of them to accomplish the task, they were like caged animals at basecamp—they couldn't get their harnesses on fast enough.

Jeff Evans

The southwest face of Everest is unquestionably one of the most technical and challenging routes on the highest mountain in the world. Sir Chris Bonnington lead a team of Brits on the first successful completion of the route in 1975, and the feat has only successfully been repeated by two other teams since then. Several other teams have attempted it—all have failed—several have died. It's steep, sustained, and has an abundance of objective dangers at every turn.

To start, our Sherpa team was positioned at Everest Basecamp (EBC) preparing to ascend to Camp 2 the next day and rotate around the mountain for the next two weeks as the heart of the summit season is in full swing. So, first things first, we had to get them up to Camp 2. I hopped in the Dynasty helicopter with Andrew again and flew up to EBC to help coordinate and discuss the next 24-hour operation with our EBC team. To move four of our guys and all of their gear would require four helo shuttles from EBC up to Camp 2. The team would begin climbing around noon from there up to the Plateau with the hope of reaching the Slovaks by dark. Then they would, based on time, terrain, condition of the climbers, and group fatigue, decide whether to descend right away or wait till morning. I gave them each a big hug and wished them safety and strength as they boarded the stripped-down bird. Close to an hour later, Andrew had them all in position at Camp 2, and I flew with him back down to Lukla where we would monitor comms all afternoon into the evening.

We settled in to our Lukla headquarters and patiently waited for each of the team's transmissions. They were climbing fast—and I mean really fast. Within two hours they were half-way up to the Plateau. An hour later, they relayed back to us that they had made visible contact with the Slovaks. Then, four hours and close to 2,000 vertical feet later, they reached the stranded party.

Unbelievable.

They found one of the climbers to be able bodied and ambulatory on his own power. The other guy was essentially blind from taking the brunt of the spindrift avalanche in his face. This left him with painful corneal abrasions. He could walk but would need guidance with his new-found blindness.

A blind dude descending Everest—I've heard that story before.

•

The team made a quick decision to start the descent—in deteriorating conditions—at 6 p.m. Ballsy for sure. We expected to be sitting by the radio till the wee hours, so we were a bit surprised to get a transmission two hours later that the entire team and Slovaks had safely made it back to Camp 2. An absolute Herculean effort.

The next morning Andrew and I headed back to EBC in a stripped-down bird. A quick stop at the EBC landing pad to drop extra fuel, and the two of us began the circling flight up to Camp 2 at 21,000 feet. The conditions were perfect as we crested over the icefall and entered the cwm. The walls of Everest, Lhotse, and Nuptse were glistening with fresh snow. We got a visual on the lower landing zone, and Andrew deftly landed us on top of the glacier.

I exited the helo, walked directly to our Sherpa team, and bear hugged each of them. They looked remarkably fresh.

Then I got a good look at my blind Slovakian. He had a patch over his right eye, had sunglasses on, and was sitting on his pack in the snow. I had him hold onto my shoulder as I led him into the spooled-up helicopter. Andrew lifted us off, swung the bird down the valley and over the icefall. We landed at EBC a couple minutes later and got out so Andrew could return for the second Slovak.

The mid-40s, temporarily-blind Slovakian climber was all smiles upon landing. I applied ocular drops in each eye, which quickly relieved his pain, and I watched him fully relax now that his pain was gone. He knew how close they had come to the edge and the effort our Sherpa team had gone to in order to safely get them down. He was effusively grateful. Yesterday afternoon they had been perched precariously high up on a technical face, unable to escape. Today, they were headed down to Kathmandu for more pain meds, a hot shower, and a hotel bed.

Jeff Evans

There is no doubt that what our Sherpa team did was of epic proportion. Their job this season was to conduct rescue operations on the biggest mountain in the world. They transcended that yesterday and took it to legendary status.

They are my heroes.

One self-appointed spokesman for the Khumbu newsfeed claimed from his home in the US that we "aggressively inserted" ourselves into the scene to perform the rescue. It should be clear that without an aggressive approach, these Slovakian men would have met a much different fate.

The summit window is wide open for the next 10 days. I'm guessing our guys will have more work up high.

And we will be aggressive.

CHAPTER 34

GO SAVE JESUS ON YOUR BIRTHDAY

Due to spotty (read non-existent) Interweb, this is a post from last Saturday.

Today we completed a 24-hour rescue of two Slovakians trapped on the southwest face of Everest. More on that later.

For now, May 7.

The older you get, the less important birthdays are, right? Well, this one was pretty important.

I awoke this morning only to remember that it was my birthday after seeing the date on my watch as I quickly pulled myself from bed to get dressed. We had work to do and birthdays were an afterthought.

We received a call last night that there was an extremely critical climber circling the drain at Makalu Basecamp (19,100 feet). The report was that he was very close to death, and everyone there was concerned he would not make it through the night. All the other important facts like age, gender, nationality, history, or chief complaint were not filtered down to me so this would be flying in to the darkness towards an unknown situation—pretty much par for the course over here.

We spooled up the helicopter and were just about to lift off as a massive cloudbank enveloped the Lukla heliport. The pilot turned down the engine, and we watched in awe as the helicopter was instantly swallowed by white—couldn't see 10 feet beyond the bird.

Just as with most important things in life, the timing was quite auspicious. Moments later the bottom dropped out of the sky as a monsoonal rain pounded down for a solid two hours. If we had lifted off two minutes earlier, we absolutely would have never made it up to rescue this fellow some 10,000 feet higher up. We surely would have been shut down from returning to Lukla, and potentially a lot worse. We were grounded and would have to delay till the next morning.

I went to sleep last night not knowing anything about this sick person that was surely having the shittiest night of their life. Perhaps he or she wouldn't even make it through the night. Maybe this person felt like we had abandoned them. I tossed and turned,

Jeff in one of the ARS birds at Everest Basecamp.

wondering how alone and scared they must feel.

MountainVision

So, this morning dawns with patchy clouds and no wind. I was fired up to get going and hopefully save a life. We spooled up again to go see what we would find some thirty nautical miles and a lifetime away from Lukla.

Makalu is a stunning mountain a couple dozen miles east, southeast from Everest. It sits very close to the Tibetan border as a stand-alone sentinel almost seeming to be distancing itself from the crowds on Everest. To fly there requires crossing one of several high passes. On marginal weather days it's advisable to start evaluating the succession of passes from lowest to highest—obviously using the lowest one possible, and only using the highest one as a last resort.

As we crept up the valley, my pilot Nischal and I kept gazing out the right side of the bird to see if the lower, standard pass was open. Not a chance—completely socked in. OK, higher up the valley we evaluated the next option. Nope—massive wall of clouds. Higher and higher up the valley we go. Past the last, highest village, Chukung—then over Island Peak Basecamp and into a sea of clouds. Captain Nischal and I started referring to our strategy as "connecting the dots." He would fly a hundred yards and then find a little "sucker hole" and take it, each time gaining some altitude. We continued to climb—now we're over 20,000 feet. I would occasionally catch a glimpse of some Himalayan giant out of the glass in front of me—just popping through a veil of clouds. We were heading for what I thought was the absolute highest pass over to the Makalu region and it looked fairly clear on our side. As we drew closer we both let out an audible "shit" as we saw the impassable cloudbank resting just on the other side of the pass.

I thought that would be the end of it and we would turn back, but Nischal, with 18 years of Himalayan piloting experience, said, "Let's try the very highest one—our last shot."

OK. Let's do it.

We climbed another couple hundred feet and followed a massive, corniced wall as it hooked around to the north until a small nook appeared. The captain deftly crested about fifty feet over the ridge down the other side. The helo altimeter read 21,000 feet. I could feel that the helicopter was straining at its max, cutting through the thin air with every rotor spin.

Five minutes later we came in hot on top of Makalu Basecamp. Our patient was a mid-30s Spaniard named Jesus who could not walk. With the help of the Sherpa ground crew, I loaded him into the helo 'till he flopped into the back floor. I turned his oxygen mask up and told the captain that we were locked and loaded. He powered up the bird, and I listened again as the rotors thwapped through the thin air.

Jesus was a very experienced climber with five 8,000-meter peaks on his resume. He had never had any physical problems in his 10-year career. Throughout the flight he continued to describe to me in Spanish how he was convinced he would have died within two hours of our arrival. He had been suffering from an extremely elevated heart rate and chest pain for two days. He told me he was losing his will to fight.

We flew him straight to the Lukla hospital where his tears flowed freely. I told that him that today was my birthday, and he had given me the best present ever. He gave me the opportunity to be a part of a renewal of life. I was a part of a team that gave him the chance to celebrate another birthday of his own.

I can't imagine a more profound gift.

Well that, and we got to rescue Jesus on my birthday.

Pretty dope.

CHAPTER 35

BE OF SERVICE TO YOUR OWN

Yesterday's morning radio comm began with an impassioned call from our team up at Everest Basecamp imploring us to get a bird up to Camp 1 as soon as possible. A close friend of one of our five super-stud climbing Sherpas was at Camp 1 in dire straits. The evening before, while carrying a load through the icefall, this mid-20's, highly experienced Sherpa had an acute onset of left-side chest pain.

The story we got was that Ongchu Sherpa was writhing in pain, clutching his chest and gasping for air. And this dude was a stud—not some middle-aged, guided, western climber. This lead climbing Sherpa had multiple 8,000-meter summits under his belt including standing on top of Everest twice. His Sherpa brethren surrounding him were extremely concerned for him as he was clearly in unbearable pain and, from their perspective, close to death.

We absolutely needed to go get him.

And here's where things get a little complicated. Both our helicopters were grounded down in Kathmandu, getting their regularly-scheduled maintenance. So of course, during our mandated four hours of daylight-hours downtime, we get a "do-or-die" mission requiring a helo evac from 20,000 feet.

Perfect.

Luckily for us there is another helo operation basing out of Lukla with a badass B3 bird and an even badder ass Kiwi pilot named Andrew. I had been chatting him up intermittently and swapping stories during the month that the two of us have spent flying on separate operations in and out of the Lukla heliport.

Good dude. Sick pilot.

So let's get to work.

Once all the operations guys made their deals and we were confirmed a go, Andrew and I high-fived and started planning. We would strip all the seats out of the bird here in Lukla, clip me to a fixed cabin bolt using my climbing harness, and fire up to Camp 1 to scoop this fella up.

I have to admit that I was just a twinge skeptical that a healthy, twenty-something, super-fit climbing Sherpa was having a heart attack. But the best approach to emergency medicine is to assume the worst and work backwards from there.

The weather was manageable with gentle winds as the patient was loaded into the bird. Then I got my first good look at him; he was sick and this was no bullshit.

The report from up high was bang on—true to the tale. As he collapsed into the helo he clutched at his chest and squirmed violently. As I went in to move his sunglasses aside so I could see his face more clearly, he took a wild, scared swing at me. He was in pain—frightened and delirious.

The last thing you want in a helicopter is to have a passenger going all UFC in the back of the cabin. I managed to get a quick exam in with some basic vitals and promptly loaded up a dose of Haldol. This would shut him down for the length of the flight and allow us to safely return down-valley.

The 10-minute flight felt like an hour. Every minute or two Ongchu would appear to pass out for a couple seconds, requiring me to press him with a solid sternal rub after which he would pop up in another confused thrashing session. The Haldol helped sedate him but he clearly still had some fight left inside his pain and delirium.

Each time he dropped out I prepared to begin CPR on him—but each time he would spring back to life.

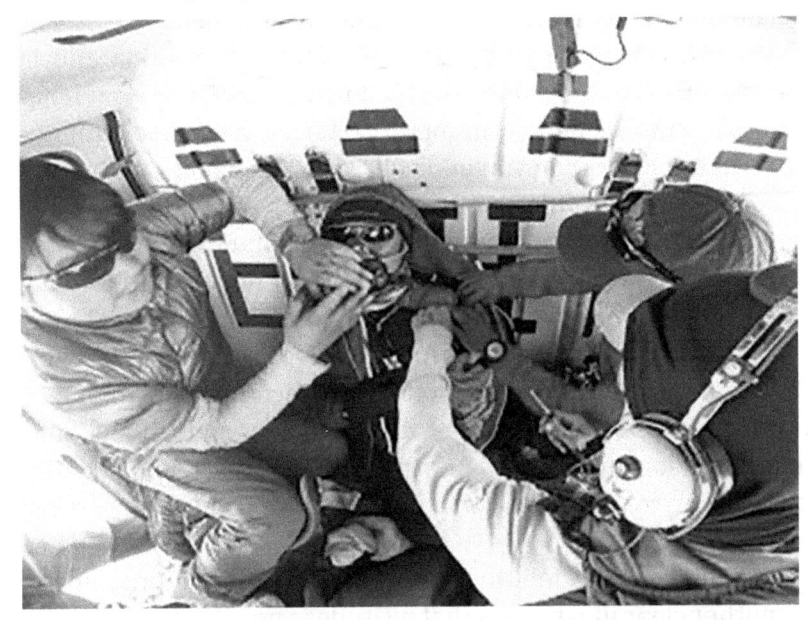

Jeff and team working on patient in back bird at 17,200 feet.

I alerted Andrew of Ongchu's tenuous condition and how great it would be to get down valley as quick as possible. Andrew gave me a choice—fly at a higher elevation and arrive a minute quicker or stay lower and safer in the valley and take that extra minute in flight time. I chose to get lower as quickly as possible as my likely diagnosis was starting to take shape in my mind, and the higher altitude was not helping his case. I began to get a sense that this was in fact not a heart attack but an episode of coronary artery spasm, which is not all that uncommon with exertion at altitude. The process is just like it sounds—the coronary artery goes into spasm and intermittently occludes blood and nutrients from getting into the heart. It hurts and robs a heart of the thing it needs the most, blood. Typically, these episodes don't last very long but my guess was that the excessive altitude had exacerbated this whole process.

It felt like we were in a rocket ship—faster than I've ever been in a helicopter. Andrew very nonchalantly radios back that he has the helo pinned. No shit. We are absolutely nuking down the valley.

We make the call to bypass the helo pad in Lukla and head straight to the Lukla hospital landing pad. I knew the local hospital had all the staffing and equipment to handle a cardiac patient and was an hour closer than traveling all the way down to Kathmandu.

Andrew requested the tower hold all other aircraft as we blew over Lukla and dropped down onto the hospital LZ.

We carried Ongchu into the ER bay, got him settled into a bed, hooked up to monitors and I officially handed over care.

Yesterday afternoon, I ventured back to the hospital to get the final diagnosis. Dr. K.C. confirmed my suspicion—no sign of a heart attack but we both agreed that his heart was indeed sick and he needs cardiology follow-up in Kathmandu today. That quick 10,000-foot descent relaxed his coronary artery and his heart began to normalize.

Our Sherpa crew felt this one. They were scared for their friend. It's another clear illustration that altitude is no joke. It's the invisible assassin—can take a strong man or woman and drive them to their knees.

I'm very satisfied looking back on this one. Our team showed how well it could perform at a high level with absolute situational awareness.

No down days in the Khumbu.

CHAPTER 36

EVERYBODY GOES HOME

I don't even know where to begin. The last four days have been a blur—multiple 4:30 A.M. wake-ups for all-day missions. Guess I'll start at the last calm evening.

The final week of the Everest season typically provides a fair bit of high mountain drama, and this year has been no different.

Hundreds of people all move up into position to summit around the same time. This is due to the weather window being fairly narrow. If you miss it, you're either stuck in screaming winds and cold or you call it and come home with no summit. Many teams feel this pressure and all line up at the same time to hit that precious week of low winds.

A number of folks get in trouble and many of them don't have the moxie or the assistance of a world-class guide to get down alive. Crowding, wind, cold, and inexperience all play a big part in creating a total shitshow. This what we encountered the last few days.

The weather forecast for the night of the 17th predicted very high winds, so we assumed that all the teams would see the same thing we did and delay arriving on the exposed South Col—Camp 4 @ 26,000ft—until the next day. Turns out, several teams went anyway.

And this is when the wheels started coming off.

The next day, we began receiving reports of 24-plus-hour summit attempts, frostbite, exposure, and severe altitude illness. We were hearing that clients and a few Sherpa guides were scattered and stranded above high camp and in big trouble. Many of those that did get down to the relative safety of Camp 4 began tearing through other teams' supplemental oxygen cylinders. Obviously this is a shitty thing to do and in my opinion, is not only worthy of an ass whooping—it's grounds for criminal charges. Stealing supplemental oxygen from climbers that are expecting it to be in place for their upcoming ascent or for use in emergencies is about as low as one can go in the world of mountain karma. It has happened before and sadly will happen again.

We were hearing that Chinese, Indian, and UAE teams were reporting that several of their members had either broken off completely and required assistance or, in a few cases, were unaccounted for. Anticipating such a setting, we had arranged for our stud Sherpa team to be in place at Camp 4 the next day to help clean up the mess and help evac climbers in need. Once the rescue request was made, our guys activated quickly. We got confirmation that an Indian woman and her Sherpa guide were "stuck" just below the south summit at 28,500 feet. As that call came in, Lakpa and Nima Dorje were tending to a sick American climber who was the client of a fairly large operator on the mountain. They worked alongside the guide to nurse this fellow back to health and ultimately helped in lowering him all the way down to Camp 2.

So that left Mingma and Nima Ninja to head up from Camp 4 and locate the Indian woman and her guide. For all intents and purposes, they may as well have been on the moon. Our guys would be their only chance of survival.

It was 8 P.M. and minus 20° Fahrenheit.

The next morning, we woke to hear that our guys had found the two stranded climbers at just above 28,000 feet. They were out of oxygen and water. Our guys provided them hot drinks and then, because of the shortage of extra oxygen cylinders, provided them their own personal oxygen masks. Talk about selfless.

The woman was barely able to bear weight and required over five hours of labor intensive "short roping" down to Camp 4.

Essentially, they lowered her 2,000 feet down a snow slope with the occasional rock feature.

As these events were unfolding, we were getting word that a young Dutch male had died at Camp 4 after returning from the summit. There are plenty of news outlets reporting extensively on his plight, so I'll just add that his sudden deterioration was another source of confusion and tension in the flow of communication between the players at Camp 4, Basecamp, and Lukla.

That morning I hopped in Andrew's stripped down Dynasty bird and we headed to EBC knowing that we were about to have a massive day of evacs and full-blown rescues. One by one, Andrew landed at Camp 2, loaded up a single patient, and dropped them with me at EBC. Twelve round-trips later, we had evac'd a ruptured Achilles' tendon, four deep-tissue frostbite cases, two altitude illnesses, and our four badass Sherpas.

At that point it was noon and the weather was starting to deteriorate, so we flew back down the valley to Lukla with the most critical of our lot. The remaining evacs were ferried down by other helos. The most in need of acute frostbite care were ultimately flown down to Kathmandu.

That evening as we are eating supper, discussing the day's events as well as what the next day might look like, we begin hearing the storyline of an Australian female climber who was in the middle of a full blown epic above Camp 4 with multiple Sherpas attempting to bring her down. I received a call from Gordo at Basecamp around 8 P.M. requesting medical advice to pass along to the team that was trying to stabilize this woman. It sounded like she was quite ill but had a solid support staff tending to her. We discussed a plan that was to be passed on to Camp 4 and agreed to communicate throughout the night should her condition worsen.

Around 5 A.M. the next morning, I got an update that she had made it through the night, was speaking, and the rescue team was very shortly going to begin assisting her down the mountain.

We had several more evacs to clear from EBC that day, so Chris and I stripped the seats from Kilo Bravo and headed up towards EBC.

Jeff Evans

As we turned up above Pheriche, we ran into a wall of wind and snow that bounced us around enough to where Chris called it and we headed back to Lukla to wait it out. The weather in this valley is to me unquestionably the most fickle and unpredictable anywhere in the world. We hoped to wait out the weather and go rescue this woman either later that day or perhaps the next morning once the Sherpa team delivered her to Camp 2.

As we sat in the teahouse waiting for the clouds to clear, we got word that the female climber had died during the descent to Camp 3. The effort to get her down that terrain was superhuman. I'm confident that everyone involved did everything they could to save her life. I had never met this woman, but her survival meant a great deal to me. I wanted so badly to help load her on the chopper and take her down to Kathmandu. I visualized it the night before. But it just wouldn't be the case. Once again, countless media sources have provided commentary about the death of this young woman. I've got nothing more to add.

The next day we heard that our Sherpa team had just arrived into Camp 2 with the Indian woman they rescued from just below the south summit. It was time to go pick her up. An hour later, Chris and I had Kilo Bravo stripped down and ready for the trip to Camp 2. As this was Chris's first landing at C2, we decided to drop me at EBC so he could navigate the tricky terrain with the absolute lightest helo possible. I watched as he crested over the icefall out of sight into the western cwm (valley) in very shitty conditions. Five minutes later he came over the radio telling me he was on his way down with a fairly critical patient.

I hopped into the bird with Chris and finally laid eyes on the Indian woman. She was not well: shallow respirations, thready pulse, sluggish pupils, and lower extremity cold injuries. Sick.

We lifted off from EBC weighted down and booked it straight to the Lukla hospital. We stabilized her and ultimately shipped her down to KTM to address her frostbite therapy. She'll live to fight another day.

MountainVision

I didn't know it at the time, but that would be the final rescue of the season for us. The few remaining climbers descended without issue and we went straight into beer drinking mode.

It's gonna take me awhile to process this two-month experience. I'll have to reflect on it and I'm sure I'll write a bit more. For now, I turn my attention to putting a bow on it. It's time to go home. To my family.

Namaste.

Jeff Evans

Jeff and the ARS Team

MountainVision

ABOUT THE AUTHOR

Raised in the Blue Ridge Mountains of Virginia, Jeff Evans has always followed the call of the excitement and wildness of outdoor adventure.

This pursuit of passion led to the formation of MountainVision, Inc. and a career which includes guiding clients up mountain peaks across the globe, professional speaking, and practicing as an emergency medicine Physician Assistant.

Jeff's climbing began in the late 80s on the rock faces of Colorado and California. Living out of his truck with his dog, Jeff spent countless exciting days scaling walls in places like Yosemite, Joshua Tree, and Rocky Mountain National Park. Mountaineering soon followed with equal ferocity, and by the mid-90s, Jeff was guiding clients as well as working Search and Rescue on North America's highest mountain, Mt. McKinley, now Denali.

Jeff's confidence and experience in the mountains led to his introduction in 1993 to blind climber Erik Weihenmayer. Little did they know that this relationship would change their lives forever and result in accomplishing feats that neither had imagined. Together, they would shatter people's perceptions about the "handicaps" of the disabled by climbing Denali, El Capitan (California), and Aconcagua (Argentina); competing in adventure races; guiding other disabled individuals on peaks around the world; and successfully reaching the summit of Mt. Everest in 2001.

To date, Erik is the only blind climber to reach the summit of Everest. The teamwork, communication, and leadership skills Jeff has honed during his amazing adventures and challenges has given him the tools to become one of the most dynamic and inspirational speakers on the circuit today. Regardless of age, gender, or profession, Jeff's message invokes a spectrum of thought and emotion throughout audiences worldwide. Jeff has appeared on ABC's *Expedition Impossible*, is the author of *MountainVision: Lessons from the Summit*, and has played a major role in the award-winning documentaries *Farther Than the Eye Can See*, *Blindsight*, and *High Ground*.

Jeff received his undergraduate degree in anthropology from the University of Colorado in Boulder and his Masters as a Physician Assistant at Drexel University in Philadelphia. Jeff currently resides in Boulder with his wife Merry Beth, son Jace, and dog Tucker.

MORE ON JEFF EVANS AND MOUNTAIN VISION

Adventurer, Expedition Leader,
Speaker, Facilitator, Physician Assistant
High Altitude Medic, Television Personality

As a highly sought-after speaker and facilitator, Jeff Evan has spoken at dozens of Fortune 500 companies and organizations around the world.

He takes his audiences on some of the greatest and most sought-after physical and emotional challenges the planet offers—the world's highest peaks and most daring expeditions—as a mountain guide, adventurer, and philanthropist.

Leading and supporting—and sometime saving the lives of — others has given Jeff unique perspectives on servant leadership, teamwork, communication, and dealing with adversity. He shares what he has learned in a natural and engaging style that anyone will relate to and learn from and be able to apply in their business and personal life.

In addition to his speaking services, Jeff also provides expedition leadership, support, and guidance services to companies and organizational teams as they pursue some of the greatest challenges anywhere.

For more information on Jeff Evans, visit http://jeffbevans.com. To contact Jeff about his services, email him at info@jeffbevans.com.

MountainVision

ACKNOWLEDGEMENTS

Throughout all my adventures I have had a wonderful support group that has roped up with me in every sense of the word, time and time again and I am forever grateful to have these people in my life.

My grandparents, primarily my two grandfathers Pop and Bish, who instilled in me so much of the balance and determination required to be successful and safe in the mountains, even without knowing it.

My parents Bob and Peggy who have supported me in countless ways, in spite of all of my best efforts to worry them. (They would have much preferred I'd taken up golf.) They have nurtured me and loved me as I have undoubtedly caused them much trouble and concern. I am forever indebted to them all for their support.

My friends and climbing partners, primarily Erik, Chris, Charley, Didrik, *et al*, who have been my brothers through thick and thin, have bled, suffered and cried in joy with me on the sides of mountains as well as on random barstools.

And finally, and most profoundly to my wife Merry Beth and my son Jace who have provided me with the love and strength to continue with my pursuits. They have taught me that all that matters in life exists within our family.